A TIME FOR ACTION

Books by William E. Simon

A TIME FOR ACTION
A TIME FOR TRUTH

A TIME FOR ACTION

WILLIAM E. SIMON

Reader's Digest Press

McGraw-Hill Book Company

NEW YORK   CHICAGO

1234567890DODO876543210

LIBRARY OF CONGRESS CATALOGING IN PUBLICATION DATA: 80-22210

Acknowledgments

I wish to express my tremendous gratitude to the brilliant author and columnist, M. Stanton Evans, who worked so closely with me on this project; to Fred Mann of the National Journalism Center for his research help; to Washington Editor William Schulz, and Managing Editor Kenneth O. Gilmore of the *Reader's Digest*, whose long hours of guidance, criticism and direction helped make this book possible.

Dedication

I dedicate this book to my fellow countrymen with the fervent belief in their ultimate wisdom and with the passionate hope that they wake up before it's too late.

W.E.S.

I

The American Crisis

... the signals flash through the night in vain,
For Death is in charge of the clattering train.

—quoted by WINSTON CHURCHILL,
The Gathering Storm

On the eve of World War I, Sir Edward Grey, the British foreign secretary, issued a somber and prophetic warning. "The lamps are going out," he said, "all over Europe."

That statement could be repeated now, with one important, chilling difference. The lamps are going out, not simply on one continent, but all over the world. Behind the Iron Curtain, where a billion human beings live in abject slavery, the lights of freedom have long since been extinguished. In the nations of the so-called "third world," they are flickering ever lower. They are even in danger of going out in the United States—where the torch of liberty is supposed to burn its brightest.

We live in a time of so many calamities and horrors

that we are hardened, indeed oblivious, to warnings of disaster. Prophets of doom have told us so often the world was going to end next Tuesday that we are numbly indifferent to such forecasts. The world has never ended before; there is no reason to think it is going to end now. Somehow, no matter how bad the situation looks, we believe we can always muddle through.

But the world as we know it *can* end—if not next Tuesday, then uncomfortably soon as the life span of societies is measured. The world of freedom, abundance and proud achievement we Americans take for granted as our birthright could come to a stark and shattering conclusion before this century is out. It has happened before and is happening again as these words are written, with sickening regularity. And unless we change our way of doing things, it can happen in America as well.

Three years ago I wrote a book* about my experience in the federal government and some of the hard-earned lessons I took back with me when I went home, a bit bedraggled, to New Jersey. For someone whose life had been spent in the business and financial world, my tenure in Washington had been a harrowing and depressing experience. A sadder but, I hope, a wiser former Treasury Secretary, I thought the outlook for our economy and the global situation was bleak. I didn't know the half of it.

In that previous book I described the forces of envy, greed, political blindness and ideological arrogance which, in my view, were leading our country toward a double form of perdition: collectivist regimentation on the home front, weakness and prostra-

---

*A Time For Truth

tion in our dealings overseas. A nation governed in this manner, I concluded, had a rendezvous with oblivion.

Since I wrote that analysis, all the tendencies that disturbed me have accelerated. The graph lines pointing toward economic collapse for the nation have zigzagged crazily off the charts, signaling "May Day" to anyone who has the slightest knowledge of commonsense finance and economics. In our foreign dealings, meantime, the signs and symbols of our weakness have been piled on with ever more humiliating frequency.

In the almost four years since I departed Washington, things have happened to our country that, not too long ago, would have been the stuff of futuristic nightmares. If someone had put them in a novel called *The Crash of 1980* or *The Republic Fell Yesterday*, he would have been dismissed as a doomsaying crackpot. Then as now we would have been told, It can't happen here. But it has *already* happened here. All of the following examples—selected from a much longer list—have occurred in just the past few years:

*In early 1980 inflation rose to an almost incredible annualized rate of 18 percent—a figure previously thought appropriate only for banana republics. At this clip, our money would lose half its value in only four years' time. (In 1976 the Consumer Price Index had increased by *4.8* percent.)

*In a frenzy of speculation in 1979 and '80, gold prices soared to more than $800 an ounce, up from $42 in 1971. Which is another way of saying that the present and prospective value of the dollar, in the eyes of those prepared to pay such prices, had fallen by an equal magnitude.

*In the summer of 1979, for the second time in

five years, motorists on the Atlantic and Pacific sea-boards found themselves snarled in monstrous gas lines or confronting "Closed" signs at their local service stations. This in an energy-rich nation where two thirds of all the discovered oil remains in the ground, where tens of billions of barrels of recoverable reserves are waiting to be extracted, and where coal, natural gas and nuclear power resources are immense.

*Numerous mortgage institutions closed their loan windows in 1980 as mortgage rates soared above 15 percent. Three quarters of the American population found themselves priced out of the new housing market, and the housing industry, with the lowest number of starts since World War II, was in a state of virtual collapse.

*Housing wasn't alone. In the past few years, once mighty U.S. industries—electronics, steel, automobiles—have been staggering toward disaster, unable to meet the challenge of foreign competition. In 1979 the nation's seventeenth-largest corporation, Chrysler, came hat in hand to Washington to seek—and get—a federal bailout.

*In 1979 business productivity in the United States declined by 1.7 percent. Industrial production by the middle of 1980, after dropping for four straight months, was lower than it had been in 1978. Between 1979 and 1980 the average earnings of American families, in terms of purchasing power, decreased by more than five percent. (A nominal gain of 8 percent in income was more than countered by a 13-plus percent increase in consumer prices.)

*In May of 1980, despite a tremendous gusher of federal spending and countless programs supposedly intended to create jobs, the number of new unemployment claims soared by the highest level in our history—675,000 in a single week. Americans thus continued to suffer the unique experience of "stagflation"—simultaneous inflation and recession.

*As of the end of 1979, total debt in the United States, public and private, had reached the staggering total of $4.25 trillion, which doesn't count some $86 billion in U.S.–held debt from third world nations that are not the most dependable of credit risks (for some of these countries, the carrying charges on this debt amount to 50 percent of GNP). Default on any substantial portion of these colossal obligations could trigger a banking panic of frightening dimensions.

This list of economic horror stories could go on and on: our massive trade imbalance; $180 billion in federal deficits in four years; continued declines in capital investment. It is incredible but true that over the past 20 years the United States has the worst record of capital investment of any major industrialized nation in the world. Since investment is the key to productivity—which must improve if our standard of living is to increase—this shortfall affects our ability to compete, not only in global markets, but in our own. And without sufficient investment, there cannot be jobs for our growing labor force—or for our children.

Steel is a good example. In 1955 we exported more steel than we imported. But sweeping government regulations and de facto price controls affected investment and productivity so adversely that between 1964 and 1977 our growth in output was exactly zero. The Japanese, meantime, have increased production by an average annual rate of 14 percent. Markets, profits and jobs for American steel are disappearing: 100,000 jobs for U.S. steelworkers were lost in a single decade.

Multiply that record across a host of other industries and you have some idea about the frightening nature of our problem. Key aspects of our economy are grinding down toward zero, while rampant inflation pushes money prices toward stratospheric levels. The projected outcome is a declining standard of living, the continued loss of jobs, more government intervention, higher inflation and the ultimate prospect of financial panic and collapse.

It doesn't take a Wall Street analyst to figure out from all of this that something is terribly wrong with our economy. Such danger signals do not occur by accident. They are like thermometer readings that tell us we are sick—symptoms of an underlying, ravaging illness. We have been doing things to our economy, our money, our business system—and therefore, to ourselves—that have caused these things to happen. Unless we heed the symptoms and move to correct the underlying problems, the illness could be terminal.

All of this, however, is, comparatively speaking, the *good* news. If we turn our attention to the foreign scene and what is happening to our nation in dealings with other countries, we find a series of events that, if anything, is even more appalling. Not since the War of 1812 have Americans been subjected to the shame and humiliation inflicted on us in the past few years. The difference is that in 1812, though we were relatively small and weak, we had leaders who thought in terms of national honor. Now, though we are in theory big and powerful, any tinpot dictator can rub our noses in the dirt, manhandle our citizens and spit on our flag—without fear of American anger or reprisal.

*In September 1979, 3000 Soviet combat troops were "discovered" in Cuba. The President and numerous other high officials in our government repeatedly said this situation was "unacceptable." On October 1 the President went on national television—and accepted it.

*In November 1979, a third world dictatorship in Iran, led by a religious fanatic, sacked our embassy and took 53 Americans hostage. Nine months later, as these words are put to paper, the hostages are still held captive. A single furtive attempt at rescue by our government ended in humiliating failure in the desert.

*In the past four years, other American embassies and consulates have been attacked in India, Afghanistan, Bolivia, Colombia, Turkey, The Netherlands, Luxembourg, Syria, Lebanon, Libya, Pakistan and other countries. In the past decade, according to CIA and State Department estimates, more than 600 U.S. personnel abroad have been subject to attack. In Afghanistan our ambassador was murdered; in Colombia he was kidnaped; in El Salvador he was held prisoner in his residence.

*In December 1979, Soviet troops rolled into Afghanistan—using vehicles provided to them by American policy-makers and American industry. We responded with mostly symbolic gestures, the most serious of which were soon retracted. The Soviets, predictably, ignored these feeble protests and kept right on murdering Afghan peasants. (*Their* embassies, for some reason, don't get taken over by third world countries.)

*All authorities agree that the decline of the U.S. military has proceeded to a point where we are second in striking power to the Soviets. The Secretary of

Defense, in fact, informed the President that we lack
the capability to project enough military power into
the Persian Gulf to back up our warnings to the Soviets. Our state of strategic readiness is so poor, according to one survey, that we would be better off
not to respond to a Soviet strike against our missiles,
since retaliation would only incur additional strategic
punishment.

*Our conventional readiness is dismal. A U.S.
Army exercise indicates that 90 days into a conventional war we would be more than a million men short
of demand and in some critical areas would have only
30 percent of trained manpower requirements. Skill
levels among the men we do have are abysmally low
(90 percent of the soldiers maintaining our nuclear
weapons failed their skill qualification tests).

These examples too are culled from a long and
dismal list. We could add such further signs of national weakness as the handing over of the Panama
Canal, our vital linkage between the two great oceans,
to the regime of Omar Torrijos; the subsequent efforts
of Torrijos and his mentor, Fidel Castro, to bring a
Marxist regime to power in Nicaragua, with the acquiescence of our State Department; and the use of
Nicaragua, again with our compliance, to launch
aggression against El Salvador and Guatemala.

As with our domestic troubles, these foreign calamities are symptoms of a deeper process unfolding
steadily across a span of decades. Anyone who sur-
veys the changing map of the world can see at once
what is occurring: The United States and its allies are
in headlong retreat, while the Soviet Union and its
proxy forces around the world are steadily advancing.
After a generation of relative stalemate, the past few

years have seen *ten* different countries taken over by the Marxists,* and others are being threatened as this is written.

These conquests are significant not only because they show the general drift of power in the world but because they provide the Soviets and their allies with crucial leverage over global resources and strategic chokepoints. Angola and Mozambique command important seaports vital to world shipping; Afghanistan and South Yemen are pincers around the Persian Gulf; Nicaragua is an alternative to Panama as a site for an inter-ocean canal and moves the Marxists closer to the huge oil fields of Mexico.

While the aggressive ambitions of the communists are not within our power to control, the question of whether those ambitions succeed or not is powerfully affected by what we do—or fail to do. The effective stalemate that lasted from the Korean War until the early 1970s occurred because the communists feared the strength of the United States and because we pursued a set of policies designed, for the most part, to stem the Soviet advance. In recent years this perception of our strength—and of our will—has changed dramatically for the worse.

Like our domestic economic troubles, these foreign policy woes are largely self-inflicted. When the world sees us back down on Soviet combat troops in Cuba, or unable to prevent a Persian fanatic from holding Americans hostage, or handing over a vital waterway under threat of sabotage and riot, they conclude that

---

*South Vietnam, Cambodia, Laos, Angola, Mozambique, South Yemen, Ethiopia, Afghanistan, Nicaragua, Zimbabwe-Rhodesia.

we lack the guts and will to stand up for our interests. And when they observe that we cannot pull off a military rescue mission, or that it takes two weeks to get a carrier to the Persian Gulf, they also conclude that, even if we had the will, we haven't got the means.

Both conclusions, as matters presently stand, are right—and both are results of self-created weakness. The decision to accommodate ourselves to third world Marxist revolutionaries has been the result of a deliberate policy in Washington; so has the decline of our strategic and conventional defenses. Add the buildup of the Soviets by systematic transfusions of our technology and the ripping apart of our intelligence agencies by Senate demagogues and media zealots, and the recipe for disaster is virtually complete. We are weak and pusillanimous in our foreign dealings today because of what we have been doing to ourselves.

If the average American viewing all this feels dazed and frightened, I can't say that I blame him. I feel exactly the same way. I am frightened by what is happening to my country, by the forces ravaging our economy, by the record of weakness and capitulation in our foreign policy. Frightened—and angry.

In the remaining chapters of this book I propose to discuss why these things have been happening to us and what we can do about them. I believe the situation can be changed—that the sickness can be cured. The medicine won't be pleasant, and recovery will be a long time in coming. Still, I believe the basic character and constitution of the country are sound and can survive—but only if economic and foreign policy quackery is abandoned.

In the chapters that follow, I examine many of the

specific errors of current policy and suggest what I believe are common sense, appropriate remedies. At this point, let me simply say that all our difficulties converge in a single overriding crisis: an almost total failure of official leadership. There is, for the most part, no leadership in Washington today—only drift. And we are drifting in the wrong direction.

One of the things I learned during my tenure in Washington is that the civics book picture of government in operation is completely inaccurate. The idea that our elected officials take part in a careful decision-making process—monitoring events, reviewing options, responsibly selecting policies—has almost no connection with reality. A more accurate image would be that of a runaway train with the throttle stuck wide open—while the passengers and crew are living it up in the dining car.

A major part of the problem is the sheer enormous size of the federal government. The central government has grown to such monstrous proportions that it is sucking the lifeblood from our states and local communities, profoundly changing the nature of our federal system. But at the same time it has become so huge that it is beyond the control of *federal* officials—at least the elected ones. To a degree that the average American only dimly comprehends, it runs according to its own momentum.

It is this enormous, rudderless federal government that is the basic source of our economic problems. Runaway spending, confiscatory taxation, oppressive regulation, as well as the resulting intolerable inflation are crushing the life out of our economy. It is because of this gigantic burden that we have been experiencing declining investment, falling productivity, staggering industries, energy shortages, chronic unemployment and runaway inflation. The American economic system is a willing steed, but even the strongest beast of burden will collapse if too much weight is piled upon its shoulders.

Even more important, this massive and mindless government intrusion is threatening the most precious of our worldly holdings—our personal freedom. Increasingly, not only units of state and local government but private institutions and individual citizens are discovering they cannot conduct the business of daily living without getting the permission of "Big Brother"—the incredible alphabet soup of bureaucratic OSHAs, EPAs, DOEs, EEOCs, FTCs and other regulatory agencies. We have constructed exactly what Tocqueville warned us against—an "immense tutelary power" that spares us everything except the "care of living and the pain of dying."

In that sense, our government today is much too big and powerful—far more so than our founding fathers could possibly have envisioned. Yet at the same time, this government is much too *weak*. We have a government that does everything it shouldn't and almost none of the things it should. Our system, after all, is not supposed to be anarchic. Our founders believed government was a necessary institution in society—to provide for the common defense, maintain internal order, see to the administration of justice. These functions are essential to freedom because they neutralize the aggressive use of force that threatens the life and liberty of the individual.

Yet these functions—particularly those pertaining to defense—are performed inadequately or not at all by the self-same federal government that presumes to regulate the minutest aspects of daily life. We have a federal government that can tell us how our toilet seats should be shaped but cannot prevent our embassies from being sacked or our citizens from being taken hostage. The federal government is massively strong where it should be restrained, pathetically weak where it should be strong.

The Bible tells us that "where there is no vision, the people perish." Other than that of certain hard-left ideologues (of whom more later), there is no vision in Washington today. There is instead the aimless movement of vast machinery, a scramble for votes and cushy jobs, an endless parade of subsidy-seekers, tin cup in hand, in search of handouts. We are drifting in confusion, refusing to make the hard decisions that must be made, ignoring the signs of danger that proliferate around us.

No one has ever accused me of being excessively pious, but I have quoted the Bible in this context with deliberate intent. I believe the disorders of our times are, in several senses, the product of a spiritual as well as an intellectual crisis. The troubles we experience are the result of a contagion that affects the whole of our society—political leaders, intellectuals, businessmen, average workaday citizens. We are without direction, ultimately, because we have lost the compass bearings of religious faith and patriotic affirmation.

I am convinced that our problems as a nation will not be solved until we recognize this basic failing in the realm of value and make up our minds that we are going to correct it. The fundamental question of leadership, after all, is lead to *where*? Lincoln said that "unless we know where we are and whither we are tending, we know not what to do, or how to do it." He might have added that unless we know where it is we want to go, there is no possible way of dealing with such questions. The pages that follow are my attempt to supply some of the missing answers.

II

Me the People

What you are stands over you . . . and thunders
so I cannot hear what you say to the contrary.

—RALPH WALDO EMERSON

Most issues in our politics today are discussed in
terms of "conservative" and "liberal" philosophy, as
if the problems before our nation are things that only
ideologues can understand or care about.

That way of approaching the matter, in my view,
is totally mistaken. Arguments about political philosophy are well and good, but the issues confronting
America today are far more basic than any fine-
grained disagreement over theory. What we are talking about is a matter of survival: whether the United
States as a free and vigorous nation will continue to
exist, whether human liberty around the world is
going to be destroyed, whether we are going to follow
rules of simple prudence in our domestic economic
policies.

On fundamental issues of this type, there is, or ought to be, a broad consensus. Opposition to seeing our fellow citizens locked up and pushed around by foreign dictators is hardly a matter of ideology. I don't know of any political viewpoint in this country—beyond the lunatic fringe—that favors totalitarian dictatorship over human freedom. And neither liberals nor conservatives—nor anybody in between—want the United States subjected to a foreign enemy or destroyed in a nuclear attack.

Certain far-out theoreticians, it's true, have reasoned themselves into some harebrained notions on such matters. But for most of us, whatever our political point of view, the need to survive in freedom is not a subject for debate. It is no more necessary to engage in highbrow discussion about these matters than it would be to convince someone he shouldn't throw himself under a speeding truck or jump out of an airplane without a parachute.

In dealing with such questions we urgently require some simple common sense. One rule that most of us learn from childhood is that if somebody is trying to do you harm, you better keep your guard up. There are plenty of somebodies out to get us in the world today, and they have spelled out their goals with total clarity. By their words and actions, the communists in Moscow and elsewhere have made it plain that they intend to bury us. They have been saying so for years, and there is no reason to suppose that they are kidding. The foremost task of the American government is to protect the nation and its people from this determined onslaught.

A second rule we learn from childhood is not to invite attack through weakness. Nothing encourages a would-be bully more than the belief that his intended victim is unable or unwilling to resist. Trying to buy off a bully by giving in will only prompt him into pushing harder. That's the kind of treatment America is getting in the world today, at the hands of Moscow and numerous other, lesser tyrants.

Similar rules apply to our domestic problems. It may take a bit of study to grasp some aspects of our economic troubles, but the central themes are ordinary horse sense: There is no free lunch. You can't spend yourself rich. It is impossible to consume what is not produced. These are rules most people would acknowledge in their daily living. They are equally applicable in the life of nations—though you wouldn't know it from our recent conduct.

America's industrial might and widespread affluence weren't built on high-toned economic theories but on certain fundamental values: self-reliance, thrift, hard work, initiative, willingness to take a risk, readiness to accept the consequences. It was because our ancestors believed such things, and acted on them, that America became the premier industrial power of the world. Economic theories can explain it; they didn't cause it.

The common theme of our recent failings is a headlong flight from these essential values. We are trying to live in a fantasy-land where we can have our cake and eat it too. We want peace and freedom overseas without facing up to swaggering bullies who make destruction of peace and freedom their full-time business. And we want the fruits of a productive economy without investing the patience, work and sacrifice that among them generate all economic progress.

Never in the history of nations has a weakened country internally been able to maintain a posture of strength externally. A great power must always provide an example of economic progress and rising living standards. This is the very essence of world leadership and the great nations have always used their economic, political and social structures as a model to be emulated worldwide.

Our foreign and domestic failures are aspects of a single national mentality. Both suggest a weakness of intellect and will. And they are mutually reinforcing. America's weakness domestically means America's weakness abroad. While the government has been accumulating power in Washington over its own people, it has been losing the power to influence events elsewhere in the world. As our economic position has deteriorated, so have our military and diplomatic positions and our leverage as a global leader.

I can well remember only a short time ago when our leaders told us again and again that America was "number one." In the 1970s, the slogan shifted; suddenly, we were told, we were "second to none." And now in world capitals one hears the slogan has shifted yet again; now, they say, we're just plain "second."

Consider the decline of the dollar in global markets. This is in part a strictly economic phenomenon— a judgment by holders of our currency about the miserable way we are managing our economy. That verdict is bad enough. But falling confidence in the dollar is also a *political* judgment on our Republic.

A nation's currency is an emblem of its sovereignty. Great nations have historically exerted leadership not only through the power of their ideas (which is always primary) but by the strength of their economies, the soundness of their currencies and the standard that these provide to others.

When a nation's currency goes into decline, it signifies not only weakness on the home front but weakness internationally. A nation so lacking in self-discipline as to debase its money is not likely to conduct itself with shrewd resolve in other matters. Conversely, doubts about a nation's military or diplomatic prospects can bring an adverse judgment on its currency.

In the past three years, I have talked at length with heads of state and ministers of finance in other parts of the world. Without exception, they shake their heads in utter disbelief at what America has become—an undisciplined welfare state at home, an international "patsy" in its dealings overseas. They look at our runaway inflation and declining production, our humiliation in Iran and our general bungling in the world arena and conclude that America's day in the sun is over.

"What you are," as Emerson put it, "thunders so that I cannot hear what you say." More than any specific error of policy—of which we have a God's plenty—what we *are* these days is speaking volumes to other nations. Our alleged leaders can talk all they want about the new eras they are ushering in, the peace they are going to get with new concessions, the problems they are going to solve with further handouts. The rest of the world sees what we *are*, and discounts our words accordingly.

How have we gotten ourselves into such a fix? One reason appears to be that we check our brains—and scruples—behind the door when we start thinking about government. Apparently, we have bought the idea that rules applying in individual cases somehow get suspended when we are dealing with collectivities. It's a bad policy for an individual to give in to a bully, take somebody else's property, live beyond his means or sacrifice future benefit for short-term gain. But somehow these notions become transmuted into statesmanship when practiced by the government.*

Granted, we've had plenty of help in developing this viewpoint. For decades now a campaign has been waged in certain sectors of the intellectual community, tearing down traditional values and the achievements of our society and scoffing at the rules of common sense. The thrust of this agitation has been, precisely, to stand the laws of logic on their head, to convince us that up is down, black is white, submission valor and profligacy good management.

In international dealings, self-styled intellectuals have gone to elaborate pains to dull our sensibilities about the nature of the communist challenge, the genocide inflicted by the Marxist dictatorships, the aggressive designs of the Soviet empire. These people have systematically told us that we should stop worrying about communism, that the Cold War is over and that we must stop being "provocative" to the Kremlin. Stop resisting, and somehow the problem will go away.

On the domestic scene, the war against common sense has been, if anything, more systematic. A veritable crusade has been waged by Keynesian economists to convince us the rules of ordinary logic do not apply to government: Chronic debt may be bad for an individual but is good for a nation. Savings and thrift may seem desirable in individual cases but are bad for a country. The constant preaching of such themes has served to make illogic and extravagance seem respectable. Since "the experts" say it's okay,

---

*Adam Smith understood the problem better. "What is prudence in the conduct of every private family," he said, "can scarce be folly in that of a great kingdom."

who are the common people to object? "In the long run," Lord Keynes instructed us, "we are all dead."

Short time horizons, of course, are characteristic of our politics. A considerable number of officeholders never look beyond the next election and never ask what might need doing other than massaging the wallets of some voting bloc or interest group. H.L. Mencken once described an election as "an advance auction of stolen goods," and that, for many years, has been a painfully accurate description of the political process in America.*

This short-term strategy leads inevitably to long-term problems. As the extent and size of federal handouts has expanded, the burden of taxes has become prohibitively high. And people who want the handouts don't want the taxes. Presto, another easy answer: deficit spending—which keeps the subsidies high and the taxes (to outward appearances) low.

Of all the examples of domestic delusion, this is perhaps the worst. Of course, deficit spending does not eliminate the costs of government; it only conceals them. Everything in life must be paid for somehow, and we are paying dearly for our deficits: a national debt of nearly $1 trillion, interest charges of $67 billion a year and rampant inflation spurred by federal pressure on credit markets and an irresponsible expansionary monetary policy.

A variation on this tunnel-vision view of politics is the eagerness of legislators and regulators to adopt one-shot "solutions" to problems without concern for the remoter consequences of such action. In the legislative arena, this generally takes the form of adopt-

---

*Mark Twain had a slightly different version. Congress, in his view, was our only "native criminal class."

ing some subsidy or enacting some program that will allegedly address a current crisis, without any clear assessment of what the costs will be in terms of taxes, inflation or other burdens on the economy. The most extreme version of this attitude is the "zero-risk" crusade of some environmentalists and consumerists, who demand that any perceived problem be banished, instantly, with no weighing of costs. What these campaigns are saying is, we demand utopia, *now,* and don't care how we get it. Such attitudes would be more appropriate in a permissive kindergarten than in the councils of a once-great nation.

The politicians have created all this, but the public has permitted it—even demanded it. It is hard to think of an interest group that hasn't come clamoring to Washington in recent years requesting subsidies, protection, regulations conferring competitive advantage. We know about the ripoff artists in the welfare, food stamps and CETA programs. But I've come to the conclusion that many businessmen aren't much better. They're worse, in fact, because they above all others should appreciate and defend the values of free enterprise and self-reliance.

As our "me the people" psychology spreads and becomes pervasive, all our weaknesses become intensified. We have communicated the message that everyone has the right to live at the expense of somebody else; that consumption has no connection with productive work; and that if people are careless, lazy or incompetent—whether they be businessmen or food stamp clients—they will be bailed out by Washington. The net result of such an approach must be, and has been, to discourage thrift and enterprise and to encourage evasion of responsibility.

An appropriate symbol for what is happening to

our nation might be Peter Pan—and I don't mean peanut butter. Our desire to achieve immediate gratification, avoid responsibility and have others care for all our needs is like nothing so much as infantile regression. And that, not too coincidentally, is exactly how "big mother" down in Washington likes to think of us: as children who cannot be trusted to think for ourselves, plan for the future, insulate our homes, operate our power mowers or do anything else that grownups should be capable of doing. We are to be treated as helpless, self-indulgent infants who need a federal nanny to look after us at every waking moment.

A people that demands perpetual handouts and regulatory coddling inevitably makes big government bigger. A government that takes over all the responsibilities of living must make a people ever smaller. Only if we can break this downward cycle of dependence can the American nation survive in freedom.

III

Where Your Money Goes

A billion here, a billion there; the first thing you know, you're talking about real money.

—Senator Everett M. Dirksen

Most efforts to describe the size and workings of government these days remind me of the blind men trying to describe an elephant by feeling different parts of it—and having no idea of the total immensity of the subject. The only change I would make in this image would be to substitute a brontosaurus for the elephant. The federal government is so huge that nobody, including the people supposedly in charge of it, knows how big it really is, what it looks like in its entirety or all the things it does.

But because of this very immensity, it is essential that we make an effort to grasp the scope and nature of government activity. Unless we understand what it is doing to our economy, our money and our lives in general, we will be unable to take corrective action.

The very hugeness we don't understand will eventually crush us. And unfortunately, there are other factors in addition to the size that make it hard to understand—much less control.

Federal budgetary totals, federal deficits and federal regulatory costs these days are all measured in the hundreds of billions of dollars. Such numbers are not only unwieldy, they are basically incomprehensible. Most of us have never seen a billion anything, much less a billion dollars. Discussions conducted in such terms are like conversations in Sanskrit. Because it is so foreign to our experience, it is hard to see what it has to do with us and our affairs.

Such problems are faced all the time by Congressmen and Senators who are supposedly in charge of all the spending. In order to make the numbers manageable in their own calculations, they treat $100 million as though it were *one* dollar. A $300 million appropriation, in budget committee markups, is simply called "3." This facilitates calculation; it also correctly conveys the attitude toward taxpayers' money that prevails in Washington: $100 million is chicken feed—the lowest possible unit of computation.

The way they think in Washington was indicated by President Carter when he presented the nation's first $500 billion budget in 1978 and proudly described it as "lean and tight." Because most people have no comprehension of the sums involved, this incredible statement went down like a spoonful of sugar. From the standpoint of most Americans, he might just as easily have been talking about $500 trillion. To understand what is really involved at this colossal level of spending, it may prove useful to break the arithmetic down to more manageable proportions.

One writer examining the Carter budget of that year put it this way: If you had started out at the birth of Christ spending $700,000 a day, every day, with no time off for weekends or holidays, and had simply continued spending money at that rate through all the intervening centuries, you would just now have succeeded in getting rid of $500 billion. Or, to put it in a shorter time frame, to spend this much money in a single year, our government has to disburse nearly a million dollars a minute ($951,000), around the clock, every day of the year. That works out to $57 million an hour, or $1.37 billion a day. All these figures are, of course, higher now—as the federal government actually spends more than a million dollars a minute.

As shocking as the absolute size of the federal budget is the direction in which it is headed—straight up. We are so used to hearing these huge spending totals tossed around that it seems things have always been this way. They haven't. *Ninety percent of this huge growth of government has occurred in the past two decades, and 75 percent of it has occurred in the past ten years.* The federal budget is like a galaxy expanding into outer space—the bigger it gets, the faster it goes. It wasn't until 1962 that the federal budget totaled $100 billion; since 1979, it has increased by $122 billion. In other words, the budget has grown as much in the past two years as it did during the first 175 years of our nation's existence.

If we simply look at the official spending totals as a share of national output, we discover that in 1930 government at all levels was taking about 10 percent of Gross National Product—and only about 2.5 percent of that was federal. Today government at all levels is taking 36 percent of GNP, and most of that (about 23 percent) is federal. Moreover, it has been calculated that if we simply keep on doing what we're doing, extending the growth curve across another 20 years, government by the year 2000 will be taking 67 percent of GNP.

As bad as all this sounds, the total government burden on our economy is a lot bigger than the officially acknowledged numbers. Add in so-called "off-budget" items (including federal loan guarantees and borrowing by government entities) amounting to an estimated $60 billion a year, $120 billion in regulatory costs imposed on the private economy and tens of billions of federally mandated outlays by state and local governments, and it is likely that federal activity, right now, is imposing a cost of nearly $1 trillion a year on our economy—out of the nominal GNP of $2.5 trillion. This is pure dead-weight cost on the productive sector of the nation—of which, more later.

Most of this tremendous spending increase has been for domestic subsidy programs—not, as we are frequently told, for the "military-industrial complex."* It is calculated that in the fiscal '81 budget, 53 percent of all federal outlays are for so-called "transfer payments"—sucking up money through the vacuum cleaner of the Internal Revenue Service and then handing it over (minus deductions for handling and overhead) to favored interest groups. In essence, this huge burden of spending and taxation has been imposed on us by the desire of politicians to "solve

---

*The idea that our soaring federal budget, taxes, deficits and inflation are somehow the result of the voracious Pentagon is perhaps the most successful political falsehood of our era. In fact, as pointed out in Chapter IX, the long-term trend since the 1960's has been a sharp reduction in our military outlays, the proceeds going to help finance domestic handouts.

domestic problems" (read: purchase votes) by giving away our money.

A good example is the food stamp program, which started in 1965 with 442,359 recipients and a budget of $35 million. In fiscal 1981 it is estimated there will be *23 million* recipients, and the annual program cost will be over $10 billion. Spending on the program has doubled in the past three years and increased 1000 percent in the past decade. Despite copious evidence that the program is shot through with fraud, ineligible recipients, etc., Congress has resisted efforts at reform and actually loosened eligibility standards. When 23 million people are getting benefits from a program, that's the way the political dynamics operate.*

Then there is the Comprehensive Employment and Training Act (CETA), responsible for disbursing $11 billion or so of taxpayers' money every year. These billions have been used to provide patronage jobs on state and city payrolls, finance "counterculture" programs such as "Gay Community Services," give money to an avowed Marxist-Leninist to "keep an eye on" local government in Atlanta and finance "outreach" workers to recruit people to get on food stamps. Also, CETA money has gone for such ridiculous projects as teaching inner-city youths to slap their bodies as "human drums" and building a steel-reinforced concrete rock to teach people how to be mountain climbers.

---

*In August 1975 I greatly offended Senator George McGovern (D., S.D.) by charging that the food stamp program was "a well-known haven for chiselers and ripoff artists." When the South Dakotan squawked at that assertion, I was glad to provide more than 100 pages of fine-print evidence documenting fraud, waste and mismanagement in the program. In the intervening years, the problem has only gotten worse.

It would be a mistake, however, to assume that food stamp or CETA recipients are the only—or even the major—beneficiaries of our domestic spending orgy. Much bigger benefits per capita, ranging into millions of dollars, are being realized by smart operators who know how to work the federal machinery to their advantage. These include highly paid lawyers, consultants, contractors, businessmen—and well-paid government employees—who are doing extremely well from the welfare state.

Consider the misbegotten Department of Energy—allegedly created to "solve" our energy problems and make government performance in the energy field more efficient. The result has been a total fiasco—from which, however, a number of people are doing very nicely, thank you. The DOE budget for fiscal '81 also stands at upwards of $11 billion—more than double the combined budgets of the *three* departments it replaced (so much for greater efficiency) and more than the 1978 profits of the seven major oil companies combined.

What are the American people getting for this $11 billion? To date, the DOE has not pumped a barrel of oil out of the ground.* So what, exactly, is happening to all the money? Researchers trying to get an answer to this question received vague responses—which became more understandable when it was revealed that 87 percent of the DOE budget is going to consultants and contractors working on such important projects as an energy deskbook and a solar racquet club in California.

All of which is the moral equivalent of pouring

---

*DOE did, however, pump oil *into* the ground for storage—without making provisions for getting it back out again.

money down the nearest rathole—with the difference that the inhabitants of this rathole are waxing fat at our expense. One of the clearest examples of the incredible ripoff that is occurring in the name of combatting the energy crisis is the birth of the "synfuels" industry—which came into being for the sole purpose of scooping up $20 billion in government subsidies.

The *Wall Street Journal* reported the lavish cocktail party celebrating the passage of this boondoggle—featuring U.S. Senators, regulators and lobbyists smacking their lips at the prospect of such massive handouts. Among other things, the *Journal* noted, Rep. William Moorhead, the retiring Democratic Congressman who helped engineer passage of the bill creating "synfuels" (sin fools?), was being discussed as the $80,000-a-year executive director of the industry's newly created trade association.

Repeat that scene a thousandfold and you will have some idea of what is really happening to taxpayers' dollars funneled through the federal "problem-solving" machinery. Investigative reporter Donald Lambro of United Press International has written an excellent book called *Fat City*—adding up all the ridiculous studies, contracts, handouts and other schemes for mulcting the average citizen that go forward on a regular basis in Washington. Using reports from the General Accounting Office and other official agencies, he estimates that waste, fraud and incompetence are costing the taxpayer at least $100 billion annually.

Examples of the ridiculous spending that go to make up this composite figure are endless, but some of the choicer ones have been assembled by Senator William Proxmire (D., Wis.) in his Golden Fleece Awards. These include expenditure of $57,800 by the

Federal Aviation Administration to study body measurements of airline stewardesses (for safety purposes), $1 million disbursed by the Environmental Protection Agency to preserve a Trenton, N.J., sewer as a historical monument, $120,000 from the National Highway Traffic Safety Administration to build a special motorcycle that no one could ride, and so on in profligate absurdity.

Waste is built into a system where billions of dollars are tossed around in reckless fashion with little oversight by Congress. Lambro cites the Office of Minority Enterprise, which kept getting its budget renewed even though no Congressional committee had jurisdiction over it, and the Foreign Claims Settlement Commission, which keeps rolling along even though the claims it is supposed to handle have long since been settled or have lapsed. Ditto the Smallpox Division of what used to be the Department of Health, Education, and Welfare, which has a well-paid staff and research budget of $1 million annually—even though smallpox has been extinct in the United States since 1947.

The total lack of accountability for such programs is suggested by the Senate staff aide who commented on the Foreign Claims Commission: "We just don't have time to look at agencies like this. We have to be concerned with much larger subjects—SALT, the Panama Canal treaties, China. We have to let agencies like this one go by the board."

The difficulty the average citizen has in understanding all this is made worse by deliberate efforts at concealment. The spenders are afraid that if the average person knew what was *really* going on in Washington, there would be massive upheaval and demands for reform. This would be an unhappy de-

velopment for those who enjoy high-paid jobs, pa-
tronage empires, plush offices and other perks of
power. It is therefore considered desirable to keep the
peasants in ignorance of what is happening in the
castle.

To this end, the bureaucrats and their friends in
Congress have perfected numerous sleight-of-hand
techniques. One of these is the "consultancy" dodge,
used to cover up the tremendous growth of federal
employment. As the government expands its role, it
simply hires "consultants" or creates "independent"
corporations and agencies to disburse the dollars and
conduct the studies, staffed by people who don't show
up on the official manning tables. Count in all these
consultants and other invisible federal payrollers and
the true number of employees is between 11 and 14
million—rather than the 2.8 million officially acknowledged.

As noted, a favorite device for keeping big-spending skeletons in the closet is "off-budget" debt, together with government-guaranteed borrowing and
borrowing by government-sponsored enterprises. Obligations racked up in this fashion amounted to $230
billion in the decade 1968–77 and are currently running at a clip of $60 billion annually—roughly the
same pace as the acknowledged federal debt, or even
higher.

In a discussion of this subject for the Washington
Star, Steven Hofman of the House of Representatives
"Wednesday Group" and Rhonda Brown of the Car-
negie Endowment for International Peace observe that
there is no rational distinction between "on-budget"
and "off-budget" items. They note that the whole she-
bang is instituted, financed and controlled by the federal government and that "where this money comes

from and is going to is no secret to anyone—except perhaps the general public."*

As federal spending totals have risen, so have annual budget deficits and the rate of inflation. The parallel is no accident, and it is one of the most frightening and potentially ruinous of the many incredible things we have been doing to our economy.

The fact that we have been caught up in a runaway inflation is known to everyone. In 1979 the consumer price index rose at an annual rate of 13.3 percent. In the first quarter of 1980, prices went up at an annualized rate of 18 percent. People found the buying power of their dollars shrinking toward the vanishing point, savings accounts eaten up, mortgage interest rates going sky high. Those on fixed incomes are hardest hit by such gyrations, but the harmful effects are by no means limited to these unfortunates.

It wasn't too long ago that various Keynesian double-domes were telling us a little inflation was good for us and that we could easily sustain 2 percent, or even 5 percent, annual inflation rates. Unfortunately, the "good" effects of inflation—making people think they have more real income when they only have more paper dollars—tend to wear off as soon as price levels rise to equal the increase in purchasing power. This requires another dose to get the "good" effect again—at a higher level.

Inflation, therefore, works like a drug—requiring bigger doses to achieve the desired effect as the system

*Still another device is the periodic uproar over raising the debt ceiling—what I used to call, in Congressional testimony on the subject, "the multi-annual debt ceiling charade." In this political masquerade, big-spending legislators ponder, study and declaim against the danger of raising the lid on the national debt—which their own spending votes have made inevitable. After this ritual has been gone through for the benefit of the home folks, of course, the ceiling is always raised.

adjusts to it. A "little" bit of inflation, like a "little" bit of an addictive drug, is impossible. Our inflation record over the past 20 years shows this effect clearly: from 1960 through 1964, the average rate was 1.5 percent: from 1964–69, 3.5 percent; from 1970–74, 5.8 percent; and from 1975–79, 7.1 percent. And for the past two years we have been well into the double-digit regions, compounding on top of what has gone before.

Compound interest has been described as the eighth wonder of the world—when it's working for you. When it's working against you, there are few things more lethal. And chronic inflation makes compound interest work against us with a vengeance. It is rapidly destroying the purchasing power of the dollar and value of pensions; it is silently robbing U.S. taxpayers of billions of dollars; and it is fatally undermining our ability to maintain a productive economy in an increasingly competitive world.

Over the decade of the '70s, inflation increased at an annualized average rate of almost seven percent. The result of this inflation rate, compounded, was to cut the purchasing power of the dollar by 50 percent. People who retired on pensions in 1970, therefore, had their purchasing power cut in half. In the years ahead, this situation will worsen. *Business Week* points out that at an annual inflation rate of 8 percent (well below what we have recently experienced), a worker who leaves a job with vested pension rights at the age of 45 will lose 80 percent of the pension's value by the time he is ready to collect it.

The horror story gets even worse. Professor Dwight Lee of Virginia Polytechnic Institute observes that, should 1979 inflation rates prevail for another generation, someone now earning $20,000 would have to earn $1,280,000 just to stay even. At the '79 inflation rate, shortly after the turn of the century a $1 hamburger will cost $32, a $10 shirt will cost $320, a $25 pair of shoes will cost $800, a $5000 car will cost $160,000 and a $75,000 home will be selling for $2,400,000.

As inflation has moved up inexorably into the double-digit range that could actually produce such results, we have been treated to an orgy of scapegoating. President Carter has argued that the culprit is the rising cost of energy imposed by OPEC. In one press statement he asserted that inflation varies with "circumstances" and "the most important changing circumstance is the price of OPEC oil, on which our nation is so dependent." Among his ideas for "fighting inflation" was to increase the price of gasoline ten cents a gallon by imposing an oil import fee.

If you fail to see how you can fight inflation by paying *higher* prices for gasoline, welcome to the club. While there *is* a connection between our energy and inflation problems (namely, the federal government itself), it is not true that rising energy prices from OPEC or anywhere else "cause" inflation. This is a typical Washington cop-out designed to keep the people in the dark about what is being done to them. To see the fallacy of it, we need only note that major industrial nations which are even *more* dependent on imported oil than we are have inflation rates about *one third* our own.*

---

*West Germany and Japan, for example, import 97 and 99 percent of their oil, respectively, compared to our 43 percent ('78 figures). Switzerland imports 71.8 percent. Obviously, if rising prices for imported oil were the source of inflation, these countries would have had higher inflation rates than our own. In fact, West Germany in '79 had a 4.1 percent inflation rate, Japan had a 4.8 percent rate, Switzerland 3.6. The United States, as noted, had a rate of 13.3 percent.

The real reason for our inflation is that the federal government in recent years has been running enormous deficits and expanding the money supply to help it pay its bills. These deficits are the prime example of Washington double-think and political concealment—permitting the handouts to continue while keeping the costs as obscure as possible. In the past 20 years the federal government has had a balanced budget exactly once—and racked up $550 billion in deficits.

Again, the pace has quickened as the spending totals have grown larger. In the decade of the '70s alone, we accumulated $315 billion in federal deficits (not counting the off-budget items). So far, in less than four full years of the Carter Administration, the federal budget has been dipped in red ink to the tune of $180 billion and will undoubtedly grow larger. This tremendous federal borrowing puts heavy pressure on credit markets, tending to push up interest rates. To ease the pressure, the Federal Reserve system creates more credit in the form of deposits for the Treasury—in effect creating money and injecting it into the economic system. That's inflation.*

According to Lord Keynes, Lenin said the surest way to destroy a capitalist economy was to debauch its currency through inflation. The reason for this was that chronic inflation sets in motion forces of destruction which not one man in a million is capable of comprehending. The evidence of famous hyper-infla-

---

*Between 1967 and 1976 the so-called "M1" measure of the money supply increased at an annual rate of 5.8 percent. But real GNP during this period grew only half as much—2.6 percent. Since prices are ultimately a ratio between money and the goods and services available for purchase, it should hardly surprise us that consumer prices during this period exactly doubled—from an index of 100 to 200.

tions, as in Weimar Germany, revolutionary China and post–World War II Hungary, in which the currency dropped in value on an hourly basis, people carted money around in wheelbarrows, barter reasserted itself and the economy finally collapsed, are grim examples of such destruction.

Equally bad, chronic inflation confuses and disorients people as they search for someone to punish for their misery. Hyper-inflation sets workers against employers, businessmen against consumers, and housewives against grocers in a constant round of angry bickering. This social effect is one of the worst results of inflation—and one that grimly fulfills the scenario laid down by Lenin.

Such confusion is a necessary consequence of inflation, since the very purpose of inflating is to deceive—to make people think they have something (purchasing power) that they do not. As economist Henry Wallich put it, with inflation, "Nothing that is stated about dollars and cents any longer means what it says. Inflation is like a country where no one speaks the truth." The ultimate horrendous results are described by Theodore White in his portrayal of China before it toppled to the communists:

"Inflation is the haunting pestilence of the middle classes. It is the hidden threat that disorganized government always holds over those who try to plan, to save, to invest, to be prudent. To be honest in one's day-to-day dealings in a runaway inflation does not make sense. To pay debts on time is folly, to borrow and spend as fast as possible is prudence. Every man suspects everyone else. I remember trying to supply my Chinese friends with whatever medicine I could from U.S. Army supplies—sulfa drugs, quinine, paregoric, atibrine—and then discovering that some of those who pleaded illness were not truly ill but were selling the drugs for the wild paper prices they brought on the open market. So I distrusted everyone who asked for an American medicine, an American tool, an American artifact. What the West called the desertion of the intellectuals is considered by most historians to be a forerunner of revolution. Unless the government can find learned men to serve it, it cannot serve the people. In China inflation made it impossible for learned men, honest men, decent men to serve their national government except for unbearable personal cost or self-corruption that revolted them. They sought any alternative—and the only alternative was the communists. Inflation had made life unreasonable."

The harmful long-term economic effects of inflation are examined in Chapter VI. For the moment, however, consider only the immediate effects—the harm inflation is inflicting on our economy right now. One of the most obvious examples is the way inflation interacts with our progressive tax system to impose a constantly higher tax burden on American citizens.

As inflation pushes nominal incomes ever higher, progressive taxes take an ever bigger percentage of that income for the government. To pick a simple example, if a family of four had an income of $15,000 in 1970, federal taxes absorbed about 15 percent of its earnings. In 1980, after prices had slightly more than doubled, this family would need a $30,000 income to be nominally even with its previous income. But at this level it will have to fork over almost 21 percent of its earnings to the IRS. So even if this family has managed to double its income, it has not

38 A TIME FOR ACTION

really stayed even. To have the same *after-tax* income, it would need earnings of $34,349.*

In the four years of the Carter Administration, this automatic taxing process has *doubled* the amount of federal income taxes paid in by American citizens— from $132 billion to $274 billion. Social Security taxes, corporate taxes and excise taxes have increased by roughly similar amounts. All told, the take from existing taxes (not counting new ones imposed by the Administration) has increased by $290 billion since Jimmy Carter came to office.

The economic effects of all this government spending and taxation, as shall be noted, are horrendous. For the moment, however, reflect on what this huge and growing federal presence implies for our political system, which is allegedly a government of, by and for the people. Despite once fashionable theories that we could regiment our economy and keep our political liberties intact, it should now be obvious that this tremendous growth of government economic power has lethal political and social consequences as well.

For openers, a government as huge as that described above is a far cry from the original design of our founders. Madison said the powers of the central government under our constitutional system were to be "few and defined." This was to be a system of

---

*Extend the process one more decade and the effects are startling. Assuming the inflation rate experienced in the '70s with all the present tax laws in place, taxpayers will find themselves sprinting ever faster on a treadmill. Someone who made $10,000 in 1970 will have to make $55,941 in 1990 just to stay even; someone who made $20,000 will have to earn $118,689; and someone who made $40,000 will need $231,024. If you are in one of the 1970 brackets listed and don't think your income is going to grow this much in the next decade, you are one of those who is being chewed up by our present system of chronic inflation and automatic tax hikes.

limited government, with the central authority checked by the reserved powers of the states, in the interest of protecting individual freedom. Today we have a central government whose powers are the opposite of "few and defined" and which, far from being limited by the states, treats them as financial dependents and administrative serfs. (Federal aid to state and local governments has mushroomed from $7 billion in 1960 to $96 billion in the latest budget.)

Our government is also supposed to be representative of the people, speaking through their elected legislators. It should be apparent that, in a system where Congress doesn't even *know* about the existence of certain agencies, the operational control of Congress is weak to nonexistent. Such loss of control is inherent in a complex regulatory system. There is simply no way that Congress can write up technical occupational safety standards, assess the purity of the atmosphere, conduct deliberations on pricing levels, inquire into the nature of carcinogens or do the thousands of other things the regulators say need doing.

As a result, the unelected bureaucracy becomes the de facto lawmaking power. The trend is unmistakable in the expansion of the *Federal Register*, the daily compilation of rules and regulations issued by the bureaucrats for the governance of our businesses, work conditions, products, schools and homes. In 1970 the *Federal Register* amounted to 20,000 pages of small-print regulations; by 1979 it had grown to 77,000 pages—and was still expanding. It is in those pages, which most Americans never read and probably don't know exist, that the actual "law of the land" is currently being written.

During the Nixon Administration, the President would hold so-called "woodshed" sessions, in which various chiefs of the regulatory bodies were called in and given their supposed marching orders. At these sessions the President would bang the table and say to an agency head: "I want you to come back here in a month with 50 unnecessary regulations abolished!" So far as I could tell, the regulations never were abolished, and the bureaucracy went on about its business in exactly the same fashion as before. So much for the "imperial Presidency"!

A government conducted in this fashion and on this scale is not—and cannot be—accountable to the people. It is too remote to be observed and monitored; it is too huge, complex and secretive to understand; and worst of all, the people making the crucial day-to-day decisions are not responsive to the public and have interests sharply divergent from those of the average citizen and taxpayer.

The bureaucrat's first objective, of course, is preservation of his job—provided by the big-government system, at taxpayers' expense. This natural conflict of interest is intensified by the bureaucratic mind-set, which is totally oriented to procedures, forms and red-tape customs that may or may not have contact with reality—and usually don't. The proper method in bureaucracy is to sign off on the proper memos and attend the proper meetings. Whether real-world problems get solved or not is of secondary importance.

It doesn't take much cynicism, in fact, to see that the bureaucrats have a vested interest in *not* having problems solved. If the problems did not exist (or had not been invented), there would be no reason for the bureaucrat to have a job. If by any chance the problem goes away, or turns out to be insoluble, the job-holders tend to keep quiet about it while drawing down their paychecks. The indestructible Foreign Claims

Commissions and Smallpox Divisions of the federal government are vivid evidence of this tendency—which makes an official agency the closest thing to immortality that we shall ever witness in this vale of tears.

The degree to which the bureaucracy operates according to its own purposes and incentives is illustrated by the end-of-the-year spending spree—a key ingredient in the constant upward surge of federal outlays. Since federal agencies routinely ask for more money than they need (anticipating cutbacks), the end of the year often finds them with budget surpluses. In order to keep from turning the money back (and inviting budget cuts), they therefore seek frantically for ways to dump the money as the fiscal year draws to a close.

This annual ritual produces such edifying episodes as HEW's commissioning a $161,000 study, on a few hours' notice, to look into the subject of "waste" in welfare administration (all concerned admitted the study was meaningless); a Pentagon purchase, on the last day of the fiscal year, of $119,000 worth of magazine subscriptions; and an order from a U.S. ambassador to his staff to give more parties to use up excess liquor from the entertainment budget.

Symbolic of the trend toward totally unaccountable government is the widespread practice of talking about "uncontrollables." By one recent estimate, 77 percent of federal outlays are in this category—meaning outlays triggered automatically by age, economic conditions, income status or other factors extraneous to the political decision-making process. Medicaid, unemployment compensation and food stamps are examples. Calling such things "uncontrollables," of course, is just another cop-out, since all such programs are created by laws which can be changed. But this rhetorical twist helps spread the notion that big government simply runs itself, constantly getting bigger, and that there is nothing anyone can do about it.

Note also that this "automatic" spending is nicely matched by our "automatic" tax hikes via inflation and the progressive tax system. The "uncontrollables" keep rolling up the spending totals, while the automatic tax hikes keep extracting more tax money to pay the bills. It couldn't be more perfect, could it? All of this occurs, mind you, without any additional legislative action whatsoever and with hardly any public debate. The average citizen has only a vague idea of what is happening and no effective way of doing anything about it if he did.

Most people have probably seen the movie "2001," which has as one of its themes the takeover of a space ship by the computer "HAL." The computer begins by assisting the pilots and ends up running the mission for them. I have no fear that real computers will do any such thing, but I believe that HAL is a pretty good analogy for the practices of the federal bureaucracy as it exists today. Essentially, the government is running on autopilot—without the knowledge or approval of the people and with scant regard for their concerns or interests.

And that, I am sad to say, is just the beginning of our troubles.

IV

The Secret System

Here, sir, the people govern.

—ALEXANDER HAMILTON,
First Secretary of the Treasury

They do?

—WILLIAM E. SIMON,
Sixty-third Secretary of the Treasury

On April 17, 1980, Americans were treated to a revival of the mass demonstration tactics used so successfully during the '60s and early '70s to stir opposition to the Vietnam war and paralyze the conduct of our foreign policy. This time, however, the intended paralysis was on the home front.

In Washington, D.C., New York and dozens of other locations around the country, political activists of the radical left staged what they called "Big Business Day." "Anti-Business Day" would have been more like it, since the object of this exercise was to whip up antagonism toward the American business system generally. "Big Government Day" would have been more accurate still, since it featured a galaxy of speakers whose suggested solution for all our ills, real or imagined, is to pile on more government interference and controls—up to and including the total collectivization of our economy.

The lineup of people promoting "BBD" read like a who's who of the consumerist, environmental, antinuclear, no-growth and anti-business movements in our society. Among them were Ralph Nader, John Kenneth Galbraith, Barry Commoner, Jeremy Rifkin of the Peoples Business Commission, labor leader William Winpisinger, socialist Michael Harrington. Socialism, in fact, was a major common theme that bound these advocates together. Galbraith, for example, took the plunge a couple of years ago and confessed he was in favor of socialism, while Professor Commoner, a guru of the "soft energy" set, has said, "The pervasive and seemingly insoluble faults often exhibited by the United States' economic system can best be remedied by reorganizing it along socialist lines."

Virtually the only radical chic celebrities absent from the "BBD" list of advisers and directors were Jane Fonda and Tom Hayden, who were, however, occupied elsewhere running their Campaign for Economic Democracy—which closely parallels the Nader-Commoner effort—and crusading against nuclear power. (Tom was a scheduled speaker at "BBD" events in California.) Jane's views on the issues are, if anything, even less informed and more extreme than those of Galbraith, Commoner & Company. A Congressional report, for instance, quotes her as saying in 1970 that, if college students knew what communism really is, "You would hope and pray on your knees that we would someday be communist."

The object of "BBD" and "CED" is to lash the public into hatred of American business and demand support for punitive no-growth legislation like the Corporate Democracy Act—which would have the federal government, in cooperation with self-styled "public interest" groups, take effective control of American corporations. While more outrageous than some other manifestations, these are but the latest in a series of such efforts. Recent years have seen a constant outpouring of demonstrations against business, including the so-called Progressive Alliance, anti-nuclear protests, Big Oil protest day, etc.

The themes of this agitation are promotion of environmental issues at the expense of economic growth, fierce opposition to nuclear power, demands for conversion to solar energy and the like. Such notions on environmental-energy questions have the backing of a vast array of conservationist, consumerist and environmental groups, former New Left activists and some of the more radical labor unions. They also draw intellectual sustenance from the "small is beautiful" writings of the late E.F. Schumacher and the "soft energy" proposals of Amory Lovins.

The emerging consensus from this constant agitation, as pointed out by James A. Weber in his devastating study, *Power Grab*, is clear: Link the issues of energy, environment and opposition to economic growth to forge a new alliance in favor of government control of the economy.

Well, you may ask, what of it? These no-growth counterculture crusaders are a far-out minority. Jane Fonda's political opinions are a bad joke. Big Business Day, by most assessments, was a flop. Why not simply ignore Ralph, Barry, Jane, etc., and go on about our business—be it big or small?

The answer is that, to an extent the average American can scarcely imagine, and as incredible as it may seem, these people are, in effect, running the country. They are doing it by methods which are not generally recognized and seldom mentioned in public debate but which have effectively replaced the system of representative, popular government that is supposed to prevail in the United States. For want of a better term, I call this new and largely unnoticed method of governing "the secret system."

While they don't get their way on every issue, this new collectivist coalition—whose no-growth philosophy would guarantee a permanent depression—has experienced amazing success in having major features of their program adopted. The "energy crisis" is a good example. As I pointed out in *A Time for Truth*, there is no natural shortage of energy in this country. American reserves of coal, crude oil and natural gas are far greater than anything we have produced to date. The potential of nuclear energy is, for all practical purposes, infinite. Yet in the midst of this potential abundance we continue to experience problems of severe and painful shortage.

The reason for this paradox is, pure and simple, government interference. There is virtually no aspect of our potential energy supply that is not bogged down in crippling regulations: tough environmental restrictions that prevent the mining and burning of coal, price controls that slow production of oil and gas, withholding federal lands from mineral exploration, a halt to the construction of refineries, a slowdown in the licensing of nuclear plants, a refusal to move ahead with the breeder reactor. All these measures are strongly supported by the counterculture crusaders.

From the standpoint of the average American, the energy shortages resulting from this oppressive regulation and its adverse economic consequences may appear to be unfortunate byproducts of policies adopted without sufficient forethought (which, as far as it goes, is true). From the standpoint of the counterculture, however, the shortfall and economic slowdown aren't "problems" created by the policy. They *are* the policy. These people actually *want* to cripple our conventional supplies in favor of their proposed reliance on sunbeams and windmills.

In the "small is beautiful" view, energy abundance is a bad thing, not a good one. American consumers are greedy pigs who have been using too much energy and despoiling the sacred environment. Fossil fuels have spurred the development of a complex industrial machine, permitted air travel, the widespread use of the private automobile, the development of an advanced economy. Nuclear energy would do similar things, only more so.

Further, such economic growth, with its supposed damage to pristine nature, is what the counterculture crusaders and the sun-worshippers are determined to prevent. The point is made by Amory Lovins, who admits we don't face a physical scarcity of present energy supplies and says he favors solar power because it *cannot* produce the abundance of energy we can get from fossil fuels and nuclear. "By limiting the density and absolute amount of power at man's disposal," he says, "it would also limit the amount of ecological mischief he could do."

S. David Freeman, who was responsible for the Ford Foundation's anti-energy diatribe called *A Time to Choose* and who went on to serve as deputy to Energy Secretary James Schlesinger, makes the point just as plainly. He says that "if the nation turned the fuel producers loose and let them charge as much as they pleased and drill where they pleased, we could have plenty of fuel in a few years. But at what cost? It would mean ravaging America to continue the joyride."

Not continuing the joyride is what this new environmentalist crusade is all about. It is about distaste for modern technology, eating bean sprouts instead of Big Macs, riding bicycles instead of cars, using solar power and windmills rather than nuclear and fossil, and slowing the pace of energy use and industrial growth. The ideal is explained in Schumacher's preposterous cult book *Small Is Beautiful*, which spins out a vision of "Buddhist economics" in which people do not use machines, there is no mass production and essential economic tasks are handled in small production units reminiscent of Red China's "backyard steel mills" (which were a disaster).

That conversion to this utopian system would mean the de-industrialization of America, a tremendous loss of productive power, destruction of countless jobs and a drastically lowered standard of living bothers the soft and smallers not at all. Most of them are typically upper-middle-class intellectuals who make their livings shuffling papers, writing books or giving lectures, have reasonably assured incomes, live in nice homes and don't have to worry about losing *their* jobs if Youngstown Sheet and Tube shuts down a plant or the U.S. auto industry goes the way of the dodo bird.

Such romanticism may be fine for those who want to practice it for themselves, but these people are effectively imposing it, in piecemeal doses, on everyone else—including countless workers and consumers who have no idea of why our economy has been grinding down in recent years. If we were to conduct a national referendum on whether we should deliberately reduce available supplies of energy, seek to de-industrialize ourselves and revert to a semi-agricultural economy in the interest of pursuing "Buddhist economics," it is doubtful such notions would muster one percent of the vote. Yet they are in substantial measure being converted into official policy by the one percent—or less—who favor them.

That this no-growth strategy and other policy views of the counterculture can prevail in contradiction of the wishes and interests of the vast majority of Americans is testimony to the persistence and ingenuity of these activists. It is also testimony to the completely unrepresentative character of government as it is being practiced these days in Washington. The continued interaction of these forces in the making of public policy is what I call "the secret system."

I use this term not to suggest clandestine, conspiratorial activity—although plenty of concerted actions take place in it—but rather to indicate that it is, increasingly, the dominant method of governing in our country today and that most people don't know about it. Most of the component parts are visible in the public record, but few people bother to put the parts together. And, for reasons that shall become obvious, the national communications media don't bother to make an issue of it.

I have called the federal government a runaway machine that functions in a manner totally different from the picture presented in our civics books. The image most of us have of government in action is that of thoughtful legislators pondering the issues before the nation, carefully selecting options, then passing laws that are faithfully carried out by the executive branch of government—with the courts benignly watching over the process to ensure that everything is proper and constitutional. The reality of the situation has little to do with this inspiring vision.

What actually happens, more often than not, is this: An "issue" is whipped up through public agitation concerning the alleged evils of big business, environmental degradation, the "obscene profits" of the oil companies, the evils of nuclear power or whatever. The issue is pounded home in the communications media until the public—whatever its original level of interest—thinks of the matter as a "problem." As poll results reflect this, suitable punitive legislation is produced dealing with the "problem" in a general sense and creating appropriate regulatory authority to handle it.

Far from weighing such proposals with magisterial care, the congressmen usually vote in a madhouse of confusion—running between committee hearings, meetings with constituents, speech-making and other distractions. While some issues get clearly spelled out and debated, these are exceptions. Often, quite literally, our esteemed lawmakers cast their ballots not only without knowledge of the specific pros and cons of legislation but without knowledge of what the legislation is.

This occurs because, at any given time, only a handful of legislators is actually on the floor. When a quorum call is issued, they rush to the floor and cast their ballots according to the signals of party leaders, lobbyists or their own staffers (many of them youthful no-growth ideologues). They do so without having heard a word of debate, read a line of legislation or even knowing the subject matter under discussion. As it happens, the particulars of the bill are often not that important anyway: What the counterculture crusaders are after is a general regulatory goal or policy enacted into law. At that point, the regulators can take over—and start writing the real legislation.

What I have just described is the way dozens of regulatory bills are enacted—and the way in which a massive body of environmental, safety, consumerist and energy legislation came into being in the 1970s. Professor Murray Weidenbaum of Washington University estimates that 25 major enactments of this kind went on the books between 1974 and 1978. These laws cover almost every aspect of economic activity in the United States, including energy matters, environmental standards, safety guidelines, product advertising, toxic substances, automotive mileage and scores of other topics affecting every American citizen in numerous ways.

Such far-reaching legislation—and, more important, the bureaucratic regulations which follow—have consequences the lawmakers cannot anticipate, involving literally millions of possible economic transactions.* There is no way this multitude of decisions can be made in the chaotic conditions of legislative debate. When Congress legislates on such matters, therefore, it generally passes a law stating some general objective—such as control of toxic substances or improved safety on the job—sets up some bureaucratic machinery to achieve the goal and moves on to something else.

---

*John Whitaker, the Nixon Administration official who took a leading role in formulating the Clean Air amendments of 1970, has confessed that the Administration had no idea of what the impact of this legislation would be on our energy supplies. "What was completely missed," he says, "was how proposed air pollution legislation would ultimately conflict with energy requirements."

The result of this procedure is that the vast majority of the real lawmaking in Washington today is not done by our elected lawmakers or even by elected officials in the executive branch. It is done instead by bureaucrats working deep in the bowels of government who spend their days devising thousands of rules, guidelines and standards to govern the life of the nation. These rules and regulations are published on a daily basis in the *Federal Register*, that fat document governing everything from the shape of toilet partitions to rules for marketing ethical drugs to regulations governing private schools.

An idea of the imbalance between legislative lawmaking and bureaucratic lawmaking is provided by OSHA—the Occupational Safety and Health Administration. The original statute creating this agency in the Department of Labor runs to about 30 pages. The regulations pumped out by the bureaucrats in the agency run to more than 800 pages. It is these regulations, defining more than 4000 standards for achieving safety in the workplace and farm—including such instructions as "Don't fall into manure pits" and defining a ladder in trigonometric terms that nobody could understand—are what most people think of when they discuss the aggravations of OSHA.

This tactic would be bad in any event but has become even worse with the advent of the no-growth counterculture. Not only do they keep up continual pressure on the government through their agitation and the media play that they consistently receive, they have, under the Carter Administration, entered into the government itself. In the second echelon of the executive departments where many of the new rules and regulations are put in final form, zealous Naderites, anti-growthers and extreme environmentalists are today effectively making public policy. Naturally, they interact quite smoothly with their agitating soulmates on the outside looking in.

As H. Peter Metzger points out in the Denver *Post*, the crucial chokepoints in the federal bureaucracy today are controlled by "coercive utopians" who favor the Naderite view on "consumer" and highway issues, anti-energy activists, wilderness preservation over development and similar policy positions. "Though their numbers are less than 100 in all," Metzger writes, "the jobs they hold are very powerful: 14 key White House assistants—including the President's chief speech-writer—come out of the public interest movement."

Metzger further notes that "former anti-energy activists are now four Assistant Attorneys General in the Department of Justice and are Assistant Secretaries in the Department of Health, Education, and Welfare, Commerce, Interior, Agriculture and Housing and Urban Development. Even more important perhaps are the Naderites who themselves control large bureaucracies and multimillion-dollar budgets in completely or partially independent agencies. . . ."

The biggest plums of all, says Metzger, have gone to the environmentalists: "Ranking jobs in the Environmental Protection Agency and the Department of Interior have gone to men and women who have sued in the courts and lobbied on the Hill for conservation, protection of wildlife and clean air and water. All three members of the Council on Environmental Quality come from their ranks. And a half dozen of the most active critics of the Nixon-Ford policy on the exploration of the continental shelf are now Carter bureaucrats in various agencies."

A prime example of all these tendencies is the Federal Trade Commission, which is supposed to look out for consumer interests and today is heavily staffed with youthful Naderites. The FTC has issued a steady stream of rules and regulations not only different from, but directly counter to, the expressed desires of Congress on issues as wide-ranging as registration of trademarks, advertising on children's television, mail-order business, and the voluntary standards system used in American industry.

One of the techniques employed by the FTC in helping guide its policies is "intervenor funding," through which the agency pays the bills for people to come and testify before it on pending regulations. This funding goes heavily to radical left and counterculture groups, including none other than Americans for Democratic Action (recipient of $177,000), one of the original proponents of further collectivism for America. Unsurprisingly, these "intervenor" groups have a way of telling the FTC it should follow its inclination to crack down even further on U.S. industry.

The issuance of regulations at variance with the stated will or plain intent of Congress is almost standard practice in some agencies: HUD, for example, has promoted regulations telling people what they can or cannot say in appraisals of housing, rendering the appraisal process almost meaningless; the IRS attempted a crackdown on private schools until Congress finally did wake up on that one and got the effort temporarily stopped; virtually every federal guideline and rule imposing "quotas" in employment or education is in defiance of existing statute law; and so on.

Where the bureaucracy cannot succeed in unilaterally writing legislation for the country, the courts take over. Since the era of Presidents Kennedy and Johnson, a large number of activist, liberal-left judges have been appointed to the federal courts. These judges prove to be a receptive audience when attorneys for environmental groups, civil liberties organizations, legal services and other counterculture agencies show up and demand an injunction halting construction of a dam or nuclear plant, enforcing some extremely stringent environmental standard or requesting a sweeping order concerning schools or prisons or other public institutions.

The distinguishing feature of such cases is that they almost always involve objectives the counterculture cannot achieve in the polling place and which go contrary to the feelings of the American majority. These people have their own particular view of what the nation needs and wish to impose it by any means available. Busing is a good example, as is repeated court intervention to halt nuclear and other types of energy projects, as was the *Serrano v. Priest* decision in the California case that sought to overturn the local financing of public schools.* Another distinguishing feature is that these cases are often brought by tax-supported legal services attorneys paid for by the federal government—in a manner reminiscent of the FTC and its tax-paid intervenors.

As Donald Lambro observes: "The special interest groups spending this money hope that, through the courts, they can achieve social changes they could

---

*Before he ascended to the U.S. Senate, Daniel P. Moynihan described this type of court ruling, appropriately, in my view, as "big government ordering itself to become bigger."

not possibly win in the Congress or in the state legislatures. Funds to these organizations are financing suits against federal officials and state and municipal governments involving Indian land rights, hiring policies, welfare reform, food stamp regulation, student rights and even due process in school discipline procedures."

It is through the process sketched above that most of the outrageous regulation of recent years has come into being. The enormous costs of this stifling interference are perceived only dimly, if at all, by the Congressmen who vote the original enabling legislation, becoming apparent to the lawmakers only after the machinery is in place and the damage has been done. The sheer enormous size of the federal machinery and the hurly-burly of the legislative process preclude the legislators from weighing carefully the measures they are adopting.

Under "the secret system," the truly vital decisions are being made in other power centers, almost all of them controlled by members of or sympathizers with the counterculture crusade. The chain of influence by which the counterculture wires its decisions around the bulk of the federal leviathan—and the majority opinion of an uncomprehending public—includes four critical elements: the media, the public interest groups and think tanks, the second and third echelons of the bureaucracy and, increasingly, the courts.

These four elements—plus various of their allies— constitute "the secret system." Together, they have usurped much of the decision-making power of the Congress, and in matters of energy, environmental policy, consumerism, highway safety and similar areas, are effectively making public policy. And they are making it in ways that not one American in a thousand understands or would agree with if he did. If the Republic is somehow to be rescued from destruction, the people must reclaim control of their government, and of their destiny, from this determined band of zealots.

V

The Media Megaphone

The press is a sort of wild animal in our midst.
—ZECHARIAH CHAFEE, JR.

In early 1977 when I was gratefully packing my bags to get out of Washington and back to the world of functional reality, I received a call from columnist Rowland Evans. "Bill," he said, "congratulations. You are the first person in my 30 years of experience who came down here, preached the message, stuck to your guns and survived. They didn't destroy you." By "they" he meant the Washington power structure, including a lot of his colleagues in the media.

A "survivor" is exactly what I felt like. As a matter of fact, in moments of self-pity, I sometimes considered survival my greatest accomplishment. When people ask me if I am interested in running for public office, I usually answer: "I spent four years in Washington running for my life—and won." There were times, however, when I thought the outcome might be too close to call. The message I was preaching was none too popular with the people Evans was referring to.

Frankly, I was advised not to write this chapter. I was told it was a no-win situation—that if I criticized the media, they would come after me no holds barred, claiming I was attacking "freedom of the press." I consider this argument roughly on a par with the view that if you criticize an electrician, you are against electricity. And I firmly believe there can be no comprehension of what goes on in government today without an understanding of the national media and the enormous power that they wield.

Before going to Washington, I was aware of the "adversary" relationship said to exist between the government and the press. But I really didn't know *how* adversary it can be—at least in certain instances. I could cite a lot of personal cases but will stick to a couple that suggest the attitudes prevailing in some sectors of the media.

One episode especially vivid in my memory arose when there was speculation that I might be President Ford's running mate on the '76 ticket. This possibility prompted some major media outlets, including *Newsweek* magazine, to bankroll an "investigative" task force to look into my background. A reasonable investigation into the views and record of anyone mentioned for higher office would not, of course, be objectionable. But this, I found, was something else.

I first heard about this venture when friends of mine in the press corps called and said that people were poking around trying to plant stories that, when I was with Salomon Brothers, I had been involved in laundering money for the Mafia! The idea was so ludicrous I simply laughed at it. Then I started hearing rumors picked up by my staff that a major newspaper in the Midwest was planning an exposé of me, including the aforementioned charge.

Considering that I had been a senior partner at one of the largest—and most respected—investment houses in the world, I viewed the very nature of this so-called investigation as an incredible smear—planting the very thought the questioners were allegedly investigating. I called in representatives of one of the news organizations in question and told them my opinion of their project—in no uncertain terms. If you've got a story, I said, print it; but don't spread smear allegations in an effort to create one.

Their response, essentially, was to acknowledge that such questioning and "investigation" were going on, which they claimed was their responsibility since I was a strong candidate for Vice President and a legitimate exercise in (you guessed it) freedom of the press. I replied that I understood responsibility, but that spreading malicious lies did not come under that heading.

A second episode occurred after I had left public office. In late 1978 I was involved in negotiations to buy the Baltimore Orioles. I am a longtime sports nut, and owning a major league baseball team would have been, for me, a boyhood dream come true. It appealed to me both as a business proposition and as an outlet for my interest in sports.

For some unknown reason, this touched off alarm bells at the *Washington Post*. I was back working in New York and wasn't aware of the paper's concern until General Al Gruenther called from Washington and advised me I should sue the *Post* for libel. That aroused my curiosity, and when I got a copy of the paper, it was every bit as unfriendly as he suggested.

Played across the top of the *Post*'s first sports page I found a long attack on my personality, work habits and service as Treasury Secretary. The author described me as a former "bond salesman" and a "political and financial gadfly," accused me of being a "darling of right-wing Republicans," derided my stand for balanced budgets, attacked a "tour" I had made to the Soviet Union at the end of my tenure at Treasury* and made me out to be an ogre with my staff. What did all this have to do with sports? Answer, according to the headline: I'm used to playing "hardball" (get it?). In fact, the article—written by a political-financial reporter—had nothing to do with sports, the Orioles or anything else except intense dislike of William Simon's philosophy and politics. If you can't destroy the message, someone once said, destroy the messenger.

As Rowly Evans suggested, I "survived" these and other onslaughts in similar vein and think it is fair to say they left no lasting psychic scars. But—as in the case of the mule that was clobbered with a two-by-four—they certainly got my attention. In particular, they got me to thinking more systematically about the media and their role in our political system.

The more I reflected on the subject, the more it became apparent that these encounters were not un-

---

*This was a repeat of a round robin of "junket" editorials that appeared in various papers at the time of the trip—one I had not even wanted to take. Any "tour" of my own devising might have taken me to Hawaii, the French Riviera or the Caribbean—but not to Moscow for three days in December! Another story dredged up by the *Post* from previous media bombardments concerned an episode when I was trying to get a submachine gun into New Jersey (I am a licensed gun collector). Possession of a tommy gun would no doubt have been useful in my Mafia activities!

usual. Others had experienced treatment just as hostile, and a good deal worse. For example, Howard "Bo" Callaway—the able former Congressman and Secretary of the Army who served (briefly) as head of Ford's election committee. In a brutal smear campaign coordinated between his political foes and elements in the media, Callaway's life was turned into a nightmare.

Based on nothing more than rumor and speculation, Callaway was subjected to charges of using his influence as Secretary of the Army to sway official decisions concerning property in which he had an interest in Colorado. A lengthy investigation in the Senate turned up no evidence whatever to support this charge—and plenty of evidence to the contrary. So, as far as the official testimony went, Callaway was completely vindicated.

By the time this verdict was reached, however, the innuendoes spread by his opponents and major media such as NBC and *Time* had done their damage. Callaway's reputation was in a shambles. He was forced to step down as head of Ford's committee and (for the time being) withdraw from active political life.*

Another example is the case of Maurice Stans, who served as Secretary of Commerce and later as chief fundraiser for President Nixon in 1972. Stans got dragged through the mire of Watergate and treated as a criminal in the media (again with the help of partisan investigators) to the point where many people routinely considered him a Watergate culprit. Yet there was no evidence he had anything to do with Watergate. Even political opponents of Stans concede he

---

*The details of the hatchet job on Callaway were spelled out in the July 1977 issue of *Harper's*.

is an honest and honorable man, but his reputation was sorely damaged by the media drubbing he received.

What explains such episodes? One thing that clearly isn't involved, I found, is hostility toward *government as such*—but rather toward those who refuse to accept the received wisdom of the counterculture. There is a general tension between the press and government, and there should be. As is apparent from my previous comments, I am no particular fan of government as it is currently practiced and think many aspects of it are appalling. A conscientious media effort to play the role of watchdog, expose malfeasance and tell the public what is *really* happening would be like a breath of fresh air.

In general, however, this is what we *don't* get from the media. There are individual reporters who dig in on major issues, and occasionally in recent years some of the major outlets—including the *Washington Post* and *New York Times*—have come up with relatively sensible editorial commentary on certain economic issues. But these remain exceptions. By and large, the performance of the major national media obscures the truth of what is going on in Washington rather than revealing it.

Examine the issues covered by the big news outlets—and those that aren't covered—and it becomes apparent that media enthusiasms and aversions closely parallel those of the counterculture. Issues of interest to the crusaders get extensive coverage, pretty much the way the counterculture likes to see them handled. Other issues tend to get ignored. Individuals and groups involved in the crusade are given favorable treatment. Those on the other side are given the business—and I don't mean stock in CBS.

Sometimes the treatment is a simple matter of choosing words to describe people on varying sides of public issues. As Irving Kristol has noted in the *Wall Street Journal*, there seem to be plenty of "ultra-conservatives," "right-wing Republicans" and rightward "extremists" reported on TV but hardly any "ultra-liberals," "left-wing Democrats" or leftward "extremists." One of the easiest ways of kissing off someone you don't like in such a report, Kristol noted, is to label him, or her, as "controversial."*

Sometimes the treatment is more heavy-handed—as in the case of nuclear power. As noted in the preceding chapter, this subject combines most of the pet peeves of the counterculture in one convenient package: "hard" energy, corporate enterprise, fueling our industrial machinery, economic growth. The combination is almost irresistible, and stopping nuclear power has become a number one project of Fonda, Nader, Commoner and Company. And in pursuing it, they have been able to rely at every step of the way on the full cooperation of the major media.

The most famous recent case of nuclear controversy was the accident at Three Mile Island. As treated by the TV networks and major newspapers, TMI came over as a colossal disaster, threatening dangerous explosions, a potential "meltdown" and a massive release of radiation. The result of this hysterical coverage was not only to scare people half to death but to throw a giant monkey wrench into efforts to push ahead with nuclear energy. If Jane and Ralph had

*Kristol's mention of this one struck home with me. After my involvement in public life began, I got so used to the press labeling me "controversial William Simon" that I thought I had picked up an additional given name.

written the script themselves, it couldn't have fit more perfectly with their plans.

At the time of the TMI accident, newspaper headlines blared such statements as "500,000 Urged to Stay In As A-Plant Leaks Worsen," "New Peril: Fight to Avert H-Gas Explosion," "Hydrogen Blast Threat Looms," "Meltdown Horror Possible." (These are all actual headlines—big ones—from the coverage at the time.) The TV networks were full of interviews with various spokesmen and self-styled authorities—heavily weighted toward critics of atomic power—discussing the likelihood of nuclear Armageddon. The networks subsequently offered lurid features on alleged horrors stemming from the accident, including the mysterious death of 19 cows four miles from the site (featured on NBC), an alleged rise in infant mortality rates in the area and the dangers of venting krypton gas trapped in the containment building.

Incredible as it may seem to those who haven't examined the facts of the case, *all* of the blood-curdling stories about TMI were wrong—and many were known to be wrong at the time. No less than three official investigations have been conducted into the accident, and all of them reached essentially the same conclusion: There never was (and could not have been) a danger of nuclear explosion, since the nuclear fuel component of an atomic reactor is not sufficiently enriched to blow up; the famous "hydrogen bubble" could not have exploded; the radiation released from TMI was minute (the maximum dose was less than the difference in natural background radiation between Harrisburg, Pa., and Denver, Colo.—or the equivalent of three chest X-rays), there was little evidence a meltdown was likely, and if one had occurred, it would not have been a disaster.

Had these facts been accurately reported, TMI would have been seen as a great victory for nuclear energy: An accident had occurred, compounded by human error, and yet the safety systems had worked successfully to protect the public. Instead, thanks in part to official bungling but in even greater part to the relentless pounding of the media, it was turned into a "nuclear Tet"—a victory perceived as a defeat.* The result was to feed the propaganda mills of the Nader-Fonda-Commoner axis, spur the anti-nuke crusade to new exertions and bring the development of nuclear power to a screeching halt.

The inaccuracies of media coverage of nuclear energy on a larger scale have been documented by a nonprofit foundation called the Media Institute. This group analyzed every nightly network news story on nuclear energy from August 1978 until late April 1979, concluding that if you had relied on network news broadcasts as a primary source of information, you couldn't possibly have learned enough to make a rational judgment of the risks and benefits of nuclear power. It also found that network reporting, editing and presentation of nuclear power introduced bias into supposedly objective broadcasts. In the case of TMI, the institute found, network coverage was tilted by a ratio of 13 to one in favor of the anti-nuclear position.

Similar misleading stories are fed out on a continuing basis on a host of other subjects of interest to the counterculture—such as the oil companies and

---

*As shown by former Washington *Post* and New York *Times* reporter Peter Braestrup, the original Vietnam "Tet" in 1968 was also converted into a defeat by panic stories in the media—particularly TV.

their alleged "obscene profits." In fact, you can set your calendar by this one: Whenever the quarterly profit figures for the oil companies show an increase, this gets played in the media in a misleading way that can only convince the American people they are being ripped off.

Between the third quarters of 1978 and 1979, for example, average profit margins in the petroleum industry rose from 4.5 cents to 6.5 cents on the dollar— hardly an enormous profit margin (considerably smaller, for example, than average profits for the media). But because oil profits had moved from one penny under the all-industry average (5.5 cents) to one penny over it, the change could be—and was— depicted, by using percentages, as a huge increase.

One of the most flagrant examples of such treatment was provided by a CBS commentator who talked about "290 percent profits" in the oil industry. It turned out this was a figure for one company, Amerada Hess, which had a particularly low profit margin of 2.7 percent in the third quarter of '78 and managed to raise this to 7.6 percent in the third quarter of 1979. Thus, an actual margin of less than eight cents on the dollar was translated into a "290 percent" increase and, even worse, "290 percent profits."

"Liberal" economist Walter Heller once said there should be two requirements for reporters covering economic and financial issues: (1) that they take a course in basic economics and (2) that they pass it. Looking at the performance of the media on the subject of oil company profits, it appears a course in basic arithmetic might be added to the curriculum as well.

Whether such ridiculous misstatements stem from bias or incompetence is hard to say, but the effect is the same in either event. Such nonsense is undoubtedly accepted as gospel by many people and thus serves to whip up antagonism toward the oil companies, preparing the way for punitive legislative and regulatory measures.

I have frequently said the media have treated the energy crisis with irresponsibility of cosmic proportions, and they never seem to tire of proving me right. During the gas crunch of 1973–74, ludicrous stories were circulated about tankers lurking offshore with millions of barrels of oil, supposedly seeking a higher price. (This type of false sensationalist reporting obviously ignored the fact that not only did we have a system of price controls but that all oil imported into the United States had to come through Customs.) At the time of the gas lines in 1979, big media outlets devoted themselves to chasing down "conspiracy" notions suggesting the lines resulted from fishy actions by the oil companies.

The Washington *Post* was so devoted to such theories that it attacked the government's own report which made it plain that there was no evidence of such oil company action and that the gas lines were actually the result of the government's own system of price controls (creating the shortage) and gasoline allocations (preventing the movement of supply to meet demand). At no time did our stalwart media investigators dig in to explain all this to the American people—or even bother to report the findings of others who did the investigating for them.*

---

*When I was at Treasury, we conducted an exhaustive study on oil company profits and found that historically they ranked in the middle range for American industry. This finding and the voluminous evidence that backed it up received virtually no coverage in the major media.

Despairing of getting more accurate treatment from the major media, some of the petroleum people—notably Mobil—have tried to fight back by purchasing ads to set the record straight about oil profits and other aspects of the business. With the networks, however, they have discovered they can't even *buy* time to tell their side of the story. The TV moguls refused to sell the time (on the grounds that federal regulations would require balancing time for the opposing viewpoint), and even when Mobil offered to pay the freight for *both* sides of the argument, allowing the networks to pick the adversary spokesman, this offer was rejected.

This was not the first time Mobil had been turned down on such a request. The company had previously sought to run commercials talking about the availability of offshore oil, its rate of return on sales, assets, shareholders, equity, etc. The networks said no. Kaiser Aluminum got a similar turndown when it tried to buy a series of TV commercials, not to advocate but merely to stimulate public thought about our economic system. Net result: There is no way these companies can get their side of the story on TV.

I once asked James Reston of the New York *Times* why there was so much bias in reporting—why so many news stories read like editorials. His explanation was procedural. "These days," he said, "people get most of their news from television the night before. By the time a reporter can write up his story, most of his readers already know the basic facts. So he sees it as his job to introduce some perspective—to interpret the news rather than simply reporting it."

That may be part of the problem but not all of it. As the examples cited above suggest, the bias is often as bad, or worse, on television as in the print media.

And since television is a prime source of information for two thirds of the people, its influence on public opinion—and the political system—is tremendous. Today's perceptions are tomorrow's statutes.

In fact, the limited time TV ordinarily devotes to any single issue gives inordinate impact to the snippets and episodes it chooses, for whatever reason, to report. An example of the resulting potential for distortion occurred not long ago on Channel 5 in New York City. This outlet featured a heart-rending report on the plight of the aged—picking two horror stories involving elderly people presented as being infirm, indigent, lonely and forgotten. A reporter opened the program by saying: "Just about every country in the world treats its elderly with honor and respect. And they take care of them. The United States is not one of these countries." After about seven minutes of propaganda on this theme, the narrator, Gabe Pressman, summarized by asking: "Are the dead better off than those consigned to a living death by a society and a government that do not seem to care?"*

This dismal impression of how America treats its elderly is totally off base—if we can credit the evidence assembled by economists Alvin Rabushka and Bruce Jacobs. They tell us 70 percent of the elderly in the United States live in their own homes, that many live within an hour's travel time of one of their children, that income levels from investments, annuities and in-kind benefits provide them with a decent standard of living.

---

*A not unusual outing for this TV performer who—as I noted in *A Time For Truth*—was one of the chief doomsayers promoting a federal bailout for New York City, intoning such verities as: "Do you mean to say you're going to let millions of innocent people go down the drain?"

Of course, even if the vast majority of old people—
or young people—are in a certain situation, there will
be others who are not in that situation—and calling
attention to this fact is legitimate. But Channel 5 and
Gabe Pressman did not report the situation this way.
Instead, they selected a couple of unrepresentative
examples and passed them off as representative—
again with a close fit to the viewpoint of the counterculture.

Cases of such media distortion are almost endless,
but before I drop the subject, something should be
said about the handling of foreign news affecting our
security and survival. One-sidedness and inaccuracy
are foisted off even more easily in this area than in
domestic coverage, since often the only information
about a story overseas is that provided by a corre-
spondent on the scene. We have learned enough in
recent years, however, to know that many foreign
policy and related stories supplied by national media
are howlingly—and in some cases knowingly—inaccurate.

Again, the inaccuracies in question are of a sort
to give aid and comfort to the counterculture and its
effort to guide our national policies in predetermined
directions. We need only consider in this respect the
routine imbalance of major media stories about "human rights," which focus on such countries as Ar-
gentina, Brazil and Chile, while saying little about
North Korea, Cuba or—until it became impossible to
ignore—the genocide in Cambodia. Three brief case
studies will illustrate the point:

—When the Sandinista revolutionaries were bat-
tling to take over in Nicaragua in 1978, they were
continually depicted as idealistic moderates, fighting
for democracy and personal freedom. Their Marxist

views and close connections to Fidel Castro were ignored. This treatment continued after they came to power. Major U.S. media outlets such as the Washington *Post* and the Associated Press informed us that the liberty-loving Sandinistas had "restored press freedom" in Nicaragua as part of their effort to bring democracy to the war-torn country.

In fact, as was brought out on the floor of Congress, this reporting was completely false. The revolutionary government kept the print media under tight control, shut down opposition newspapers and prevented the expression of contrary opinion on radio and television. This was part and parcel of a widespread effort at Marxist brainwashing assisted by the Cubans and supported by the Soviets, including indoctrination programs in the schools.

—During debate over the Panama Canal treaties, ABC television reporter Geraldo Rivera filed news features from Panama concerning conditions in the country and the attitudes of the Panamanian people. On his return, Rivera openly confessed that his stories had been deliberately slanted to assist the passage of the treaties.

In an interview with *Playboy,* Rivera revealed that he had been roughed up by General Torrijos' goon squads, saw radical Panamanians running amok and perceived that the Torrijos government was generally repressive. Yet he decided *not* to report these things, he said, because to do so would have endangered passage of the treaties.

"The vote was so close at that point," he explained, "it could have gone either way, and I knew while I was down there that if I continually focused on the radicals and the suppression by Torrijos of political activists within his country, I might be in part responsible for the Senate's rejection of the treaty, which would probably have led to physical violence and bloodshed."

Though he was himself "belted around" by Torrijos' National Guard, Rivera added, "we really played the whole thing very mellow . . . we downplayed the whole incident. That was the day I decided that I had to be very careful about what I said because I would defeat the very thing that I wanted to achieve. Later I had dinner with some people from the New York *Times* and Washington *Post*, and we all felt the same way."

—One of the major counterculture efforts on the foreign policy scene is the destruction of our Central Intelligence Agency. Among the cooperative gestures of the media was a three-part series on the Public Broadcast System this year entitled "On Company Business." This was a blast against the CIA as viewed from the standpoint of renegade agent Philip Agee, who has made a career of exposing CIA case officers and trying to bring the agency down in ruins.

At no point in this PBS series was it pointed out that Agee, far from objecting to intelligence practices generally, condemns only those of the CIA—not the Soviet KGB. In fact, Agee told an interviewer in 1975 that "the CIA is on the wrong side, that is, the capitalistic side. I approve KGB activities, communist activities in general, when they are to the advantage of the oppressed." This is the man whose propaganda was disseminated on tax-supported public television —without informing the American public of his true allegiances.

As all these items suggest, our "right to know," as exercised through many of the national media, is strangely selective. We are entitled to endless exposés on such items as Watergate, the alleged evils of nuclear power, the inner workings of the CIA and so on—exposes often as false as they are relentless. Concerning issues that cut the other way, however, we are given almost no information, or provided with data that are inaccurate. A "Bo" Callaway or Maurice Stans will be ripped to shreds on the basis of false accusations, but the *truth* about the stated purposes of a Jane Fonda or Philip Agee is studiously not reported.

The issue here, obviously, is more than fairness or unfairness to particular individuals, although such judgments are important. The point is that the media, by such behavior, are warping the political system beyond all recognition. They have become an integral, active force in that system—in some ways the most powerful force of all. They are not merely "reporting" news but actively involved in making it (or suppressing it), then solemnly passing the results along to the American people as "the way it is."

One obvious consequence of such lopsided treatment is to make it less likely that the people of merit and stature who do not share the values being pounded home by the media will be willing to accept official service. The end result must be to ensure that people staffing the government are either those who have no discernible policy views to set the media on their trail or else are actively working for the counterculture program. At the end of this road, if we don't stop savaging our public servants, we are going to wind up with a government run by academics or neuters— or by people totally committed to pushing us even further toward calamity. As George Shultz put it in a recent address: "Right now, the general view seems to be that anyone who serves in the government should have his head examined. Or, barring that, he is fair game to have everything else about him examined. What's more, he is presumed to have a sinister conflict of interest if he happens to know anything about his area of reponsibility on the basis of prior experience. Unless this atmosphere is changed, business people cannot make the contributions to government operations that many of them want to make and can make."

In a system that is supposed to be based on public opinion—and still requires some form of popular consent to function—the media wield a tremendous power. Within broad limits, they can decide what our political debates will be about, what "the issues" are (nuclear power, pollution, the evils of the CIA) and what they are *not* (government responsibility for energy problems, the failings of a Torrijos, the true character of Philip Agee). In effect, they set the agenda of the debate, jump in to help one side and attack the other, then stand back to declare the winners and the losers of the contest.

A few months back there was a furor over the showing on public television of a program called "Death of a Princess," concerning the execution of a princess in the Saudi Arabian royal family. At the time, I happened to be talking in London with a member of the Saudi royal family, who thought the program was unfair and harmful and was protesting its showing. I told him I understood their concern and thought this so-called docudrama was in bad taste and that the network had shown exceedingly bad judgment in airing it, but that I would forever defend the right of American broadcasters to show such a presentation. I didn't expect the people in Saudi Arabia to understand our viewpoint, I said, but a free press is critically important to the survival of all our American freedoms.*

As indicated, I think we need a much more vigorous media effort in reporting the misdeeds of government. but many in the media are creating conditions that are hazardous to press freedom. By constantly pushing the country toward collectivist regimentation, they are creating a controlled society which can affect press freedoms as well as others.

It is worth recalling that despite their power to affect opinion, the media are not held in particularly high esteem by the American public. If the idea takes root that society should be closely regulated and that business institutions should be subjected to punitive government control, there is no reason to think the media themselves will escape such treatment. All of them, after all, are businesses. Freedom is indivisible, and media spokesmen who have been working overtime to deny liberty to others may someday discover that they have forfeited their own.

---

*Having said this, I might add that tax-supported public broadcasting is itself an anomaly in a free society.

VI

Only the Big Survive

The American people are the only animal that can be skinned more than once.

—19TH CENTURY WESTERN SAYING

At a meeting of large Republican business contributors in Ft. Lauderdale in 1976, I was called upon to extol the virtues of free enterprise and limited government—themes with which big business types are usually quite comfortable (up to a point).

My rip-snorting free market rhetoric seemed to be going over nicely until I went too far—to the subject of trucking regulation. Under a free enterprise system, I said, there should be vigorous competition to serve consumers, not the existing rigmarole of limited entry, route restrictions and collusive rate-making, all of which hold prices high and scalp consumers.

All of a sudden, I found, my free market views were not so popular anymore, at least with some of my listeners. After I finished, a portly type arose in the back of the room. "I run one of the largest trucking fleets in the Southeast," he said. "Sounds to me like your proposals would put me out of business. Why should I support you and your party?"

Why indeed? Here was a "free enterprise" businessman benefiting from regulation that stifled competition, and he wanted that regulation to stay right where it was. In terms of his own economic self-interest, deregulation and free markets were the last things he wanted to hear about. I had an answer for him, however: First, he didn't have to worry about me, because I was stepping down from government at the end of the year, whatever the outcome of the election. Second, our political stalwarts in the Congress would never have the courage to abolish trucking regulation anyway!*

I recall this episode not only to illustrate that some business people have a double standard where government is concerned—which is certainly true—but to make a deeper point: namely, that the existing tangle of governmental regulation, allegedly put in place to protect the little guy and serve consumers, often does the opposite. In fact, it is almost always those who are *already powerful* who benefit from economic regulation. And there is plenty of evidence that government interference in other areas—health, safety, the environment—has a similar counterproductive impact.

This reverse-English effect stems from three interrelated aspects of government activity:

---

*In 1980 a watered down version of trucking deregulation did get passed, after having been heavily compromised under pressure from the industry. As the New York *Times* observed, "The law nibbles at abuses when it should chop away the waste inherent in trying to run a $50 billion industry by federal fiat."

First, the big guys are better able to withstand the massive costs of regulation by deploying or hiring staff to handle compliance and by spreading increased capital costs and operating outlays over a larger volume of production—meaning lower costs per unit.

Second, big government as practiced today is a vast influence system yielding results for those who know how to manipulate the levers of power. This automatically favors those with money, know-how and connections, which means the established "big guys," not the fledgling little ones attempting to get started.

Third, the dynamics of the political system favor groups that are concentrated and actively involved in the regulatory process, with high stakes in the outcome of some specific bureaucratic decision. Such people consistently prevail over those who are dispersed and far from the regulatory system, with a small stake in any given decision (although a big stake in the overall process)—in other words, America's consumers.

Put all these factors together and you have a perfect formula for victimizing little guys, enhancing the power of the big operators, and achieving economic effects that are the opposite of what we have been promised. The fact that all of this is advertised as the workings of a "compassionate" government is one of the greatest frauds in the history of American politics.

Start with the massive costs imposed by constantly increasing regulatory demands, paperwork requirement, capital outlays for pollution control, etc., etc.—the $120 billion that business has to spend each year in order to meet governmental regulatory requirements. Such massive expenses are not easy for any firm to absorb, but they are obviously more difficult for small firms than large ones.

A good example is the "ERISA" pension reform adopted by Congress in 1974. This bill required business firms offering pensions to their employes to observe procedures and provide benefit guarantees comparable to the largest corporations. Obviously, such requirements were difficult for small companies to meet, and many of these simply terminated their pension plans as a result (7300 plans were abandoned in 1976, an 84 percent increase over 1975).

Similar results followed adoption of the Food and Drug Amendments of 1962, vastly increasing the amount of documentation required to certify new pharmaceuticals. The average cost to certify a new drug under these requirements increased from about $2 million in 1962 to $54 million in 1978. Only the largest of pharmaceutical companies have been able to absorb this burden and forge ahead with innovations—with the result, according to a study from Duke University, that drug innovations have become increasingly concentrated in the larger pharmaceutical houses.

The recent troubles of the auto industry also make the point. While all auto manufacturers are suffering from a combination of economic ills, including excessive government regulation, it was the smallest and shakiest of the "Big Three"—Chrysler—that was the first to go down. Although I am no defender of Chrysler management—and opposed the federal bailout—it is obvious that, because the company had a volume only one fourth the size of GM's, per-unit production costs required by regulation were much higher—$620 compared to GM's $340. To meet GM's price competition per unit, Chrysler had to settle for a smaller margin per vehicle.

What is true of regulatory costs in general is also

true of specific types of regulation. So-called "protective" regulations in the field of transportation, financial institutions, communications, etc., have the effect of guarding developed, powerful interests already in the field and heading off competition from fledgling entrants who might lure business from the big boys.

A flagrant instance of stacking the deck against the little guy is Regulation Q of the Federal Reserve System. The self-evident effect of this regulation, holding passbook interest rates to less than 6 percent, is to euchre small savers out of billions of dollars—as much as $75 billion a year, according to one estimate. With inflation and market interest rates in double digits, this limitation on small savers is nothing short of highway robbery.

Large savers are not similarly afflicted. Being more conversant with what is happening in credit markets, they would not sit still for an 8 percent *loss* on their money, which is roughly what small savers experienced in 1979. Larger depositors who could manage big-ticket certificates were therefore able to get something closer to market rates of interest. The big guys survive, while the little ones perish.*

Protecting the big guys has been the object of transit regulation from the beginning. As the Interstate Commerce Commission once put it, its policy historically has been "to protect already authorized car-

*Under a complex, slow-moving "reform," Q is now supposed to be phased out. The effect of this measure is summed up by Rep. Fernand St Germain (D., R.I.): "The poor consumers who had hoped for a simple and more profitable means of saving now must have a calculator, a knowledge of the tides, an astrologer, a psychic, a CPA, an investment counselor and legal counsel to determine how best to deposit their meager savings."

riers from unintended or unwarranted competition."
The Civil Aeronautics Board once voiced a similar
view, asserting: "We recognize that some competition
between local service carriers and trunk lines (major
air carriers) is inevitable, but we intend not only to
minimize such competition but to prevent its development to the greatest feasible extent."*   These statements have been fully borne out by experience.

Item. When the CAB was founded in 1938, there
were 19 trunk lines serving large American cities.
Forty years later, there were 11. In this span of four
decades—a period of explosive growth in air travel
and exciting new technological developments in aviation—not a single new major carrier was certified by
CAB. Smaller non-scheduled airlines that arose to
give competition in the 1940s were relentlessly driven
to the wall and limited in the service they could provide. Only in geographically large states like California and Texas were smaller independents able to
compete effectively since CAB authority did not extend to intrastate airlines.

Item. The Federal Communications Commission
has authority over broadcast licensing, allegedly to
divide up frequencies and avoid "jamming" of the
airwaves. Beginning in 1966, however, it asserted its
authority over the infant Cable TV industry—which
doesn't use the airwaves and doesn't get involved in
"jamming"—to freeze its development in the 100 largest markets in the United States. This move was made
strictly to protect the interests of the networks, their
owned stations and their affiliates, which as a result
enjoyed cartel-like benefits in all these cities. Only

---

*These attitudes have been altered, I am glad to say, by recent
pressures for deregulation at both agencies.

recently has the regulatory death grip on Cable TV been relaxed.

Item. In the middle 1960s, Joe Jones of Atlanta, a black man with experience in the trucking business, applied to the ICC for an operating license to run truck service between the South and Northern cities. This request was routinely denied on the grounds that existing truck lines were providing all the service that was needed. (After an outcry in Jones's behalf, this denial was reversed.) The turndown was par for the course in trucking regulation—where entry has been strictly limited, routes apportioned on a monopolistic basis and rates collusively set with the approval of the government.

These examples could be multiplied repeatedly throughout the economy wherever federal, state or local economic regulation has taken hold. The ultimate loser from such manipulations, of course, is the consumer. Open competition and free entry lead to innovations in product quality and efficiency, better service and lower prices. Where such competition is prevented, the pace of innovation is slowed, and consumer prices are held above the level where the market would set them (which is the very point of preventing competition).

Consider the case of the Big John boxcar Southern Railways tried to introduce in 1961 to permit more efficient and lower-cost handling of grain. Because of the efficiencies of operation that this new boxcar permitted, Southern requested permission from the ICC to reduce its grain haulage rates by 60 percent. This was loudly protested by the truckers and the barge lines who didn't want such low-price competition, and it was only after a four-year battle before the ICC and the courts that Southern was able to get this rate decrease accepted—resulting in lower grain, milk and poultry prices for consumers in its service area.

Keeping prices up is, basically, what transportation regulation is all about, and any suggestion of competitive rate-cutting is guaranteed to cause protests and dithering from competitive carriers. A prize example occurred in the 1960s when a disgusted trucker in Nebraska sent the ICC a proposed rate for hauling "yak fat"—a fictional commodity. This immediately caused competitors to protest that he couldn't *really* haul yak fat at that price and set off rounds of deep deliberations as to whether the proposed rate for hauling nonexistent yak fat was "destructive competition." Nothing could better illustrate the absurdity of the whole price-fixing game.

Where prices in regulated versus non-regulated segments of the same industry can be compared, they are almost always lower in the non-regulated categories. It was found that air carriers operating entirely within the boundaries of California or Texas, and thus immune from the CAB's tender mercies with respect to rates, had fare levels approximately 50 percent lower than those certified by the CAB.* Similarly, agricultural commodities carried by truck (exempt from ICC rate regulation) moved at prices substantially lower than those for regulated commodities.

Higher prices are only one of the costs consumers have to bear because of government suppression of competition and innovation. Since the introduction

---

*Even today, the traveler flying the intrastate PSA from Los Angeles to San Francisco, a distance of 337 miles, pays $53, with a limited number of seats available at $35. A passenger on Eastern Airlines' much shorter route New York–Washington shuttle (distance: 203 miles) pays $60.

of the 1962 drug amendments, for example, the rate of introduction of new therapeutic drugs in the United States has been cut in half, and the United States, once a leader in this field, now brings up the rear. As a result, many life-saving drugs for treating heart disease, hypertension, asthma and other diseases that are available in England, France and other nations and not available to Americans.

How many people have died in America because drugs useful in treating heart disease available in other countries are not accessible in this country? Dr. William Wardell of the University of Rochester puts the number of coronary deaths at 10,000 a year. Professor Sam Peltzman of UCLA has estimated that the harm inflicted by the 1962 amendments far outweighs whatever marginal good they may have accomplished. It is doubtful that if penicillin were introduced today— or aspirin—either could survive the obstacle course erected by the FDA.

Other counterproductive consequences in the field of health care have followed from federal intervention. Direct subsidy programs such as Medicare and Medicaid and federal tax treatment of health insurance plans have radically tilted our medical economy toward a system of third-party payment—in which someone other than the patient picks up the tab (90-plus percent of hospital bills are handled on this basis, 55 percent of them paid for by the federal government).

Unsurprisingly, in the decade after adoption of Medicare and Medicaid, health care spending went through the roof: Hospital charges rose by 300 percent in the decade, while consumer prices generally were increasing by 75 percent. The medical "cost explosion" that the federal regulators now want to "contain" by bureaucratic fiat is itself a creation of the federal government.

The negative logic of federal health and other interventionist programs is dictated by political considerations. If the FDA were to approve the sale of a drug that resulted in the death of one person, the political outcry would be deafening because the issue would be spotlighted and the cause of death specifically known. But the death of tens of thousands of people because the FDA has not permitted the marketing of beneficial drugs is not attributed to the FDA. Given that imbalance, the bureaucratic deck is stacked in favor of denying new drug applications.

Such bias toward the visible and immediate and indifference to less visible, remote but equally valid considerations marks the whole world of regulation. As noted, there has been a tremendous outcry against nuclear power even though there has never been a death from the peaceful use of nuclear energy—because nuclear plants are highly visible and have been spotlighted for controversy by the campaigns of the counterculture. But, as Professor Petr Beckmann points out, the *absence* of nuclear power results in numerous health hazards since this forces greater reliance on more dangerous energy sources, including coal, petroleum and natural gas.

The new "social" regulation favored by the counterculture and implemented by such agencies as the EPA, the Consumer Product Safety Commission, OSHA, etc., differs from the old "economic" regulation in that it cuts across industry lines and is characterized by a general hostility to business rather than being captive to some segment of it. That distinction, however, does little to make it more beneficial for consumers. On the track record, in fact, this "social" regulation is just as harmful in terms of price and counterproductive consequences in the realm of health and safety as the old-fangled economic kind.

Housing offers a prime example. There have always been building, safety and other regulations in the housing field. But the past decade has witnessed an explosion of new "environmental" regulations mandating energy standards, specific types of insulation, underground wiring and low-density construction requiring permits from literally dozens of state, local and federal agencies. This process has increased the capital costs of building and greatly prolonged construction schedules—from a period of months to, now, a period of years. New housing costs, as a result, have increased in geometric proportion.

Because of this regulation—interacting with inflation-driven mortgage rates—the vast majority of Americans has been priced right out of the new home market. In 1970, according to data compiled by the National Association of Home Builders, 47.7 percent of the nation's families could afford a median-priced new home. By 1979, the number was down to 23.5 percent. This fits the program of the "no growth" crusaders to a T. As Professor Bernard Frieden has demonstrated, the object of much so-called "environmental" regulation in this area is to freeze out the riffraff by making development standards and costs prohibitively high. (Among the mandated features of one new housing development in California: ramps for migrating salamanders to walk on.)

Such crushing economic costs might be acceptable if they were really the price of improving the environment, but there is precious little evidence that this is so. In fact, a lot of this one-eyed regulation actually *damages* the environment. The classic case is the ban on DDT, a compound which has saved millions of lives by suppressing disease and increasing agricultural yields around the world and has never, so far as is known, been the cause of a single human death. With the crackdown on DDT, millions of acres of crops and forest land have been stripped by insects, malaria has staged a global comeback, and numerous pesticides have been marketed as substitutes that are far more lethal for human beings (but safer for insects).

Such results are almost inevitable with a regulatory mind-set that fixes on a single do-it-now objective without considering the costs or consequences. Similar things occurred when non-lethal phosphate detergents were replaced with caustic—and dangerous—cleaning compounds. Or when catalytic converters were forced into automobiles to reduce tailpipe emissions and themselves emitted dangerous fumes. Or when a hurry-up order of the Consumer Product Safety Commission requiring flame-proofing of children's sleepwear resulted in millions of garments being treated with a chemical called Tris—which turned out to be a carcinogen.

Not counting the costs or consequences of regulatory actions involves more than dollars and cents. It involves unforeseen impact on health, safety, and the environment and economic growth beyond the immediate visible effect of a given action—impacts that the regulators in their blinders-on fixation with single objectives refuse to consider. The question is not dollars versus lives—but lives versus lives. And the evidence is good that, in addition to imposing enormous dollar costs on the economy, the regulators are actually blighting and destroying lives rather than enhancing or saving them. Again we are dealing with an almost childlike mentality that seeks a quick fix now without considering remoter implications.

Obviously, massive outlays to force the sifting out of every last particle of soot from smoke stacks will reduce the amounts of soot from smoke stacks. But the health and safety benefits from all this massive regulation are, to put it mildly, elusive. There is no evidence, for example, that OSHA, with all its thousands of workplace standards, has actually improved occupational safety. In fact, man-days lost on the job because of accidents actually increased after OSHA went into operation (from 53.3 per 100 workers in 1973 to 61.6 in 1977).

The common feature of OSHA regs, EPA "zero discharge" crusades and NHTSA efforts to improve traffic safety is that they seek to create a risk-free existence by manipulating objects. But most accidents and other health and safety hazards—an estimated 85 percent of traffic accidents, for example—result from human error or carelessness. The crusade to create a totally risk-free environment or packaged life for human beings is therefore doomed to failure from the outset.

A dawning awareness of this and other regulatory problems has begun to show itself in Washington and certain sectors of the academic community. Even a few confirmed statists like Teddy Kennedy and Ralph Nader have, for various reasons, acknowledged the problems of the "old" regulation and helped push for deregulatory initiatives in air travel, trucking and financial institutions. Professor Charles Schultze of the Brookings Institution and chairman of President Carter's Council of Economic Advisers has argued that top-down "command and control" regulation of the type pursued by OSHA doesn't work and that market incentives are preferable to such regulation.

Unfortunately, while this perception of regulatory failure has caught up to the CAB and the ICC, it has not yet made its impact felt on EPA, CPSC, OSHA and some of the other "new breed" regulatory agencies. Nor has it done much to slow the overall growth of government powers—where the imperatives of "structuralism" prevail. When it turns out that the massive structure put in place to regulate us into utopia can't really get the job done, hardly anyone steps forward to say the structure should be phased out. Instead, new purposes are invented for it.

The overriding new objective of big government these days is "income transfer"—leveling out disparities in wealth in the economy. Taking from the well-to-do and giving to the needy is the new goal of federal social policy, and as a result, the "transfer payment" segment of the federal budget has grown enormously. Such leveling has its own negative consequences and is of questionable propriety in a system allegedly devoted to individual freedom and responsibility and to the ideals of limited government.

Even assuming such a program is legitimate, however, we can again raise the question of whether federal policy is actually doing what the advertising says—whether the "little" guy is being helped at the expense of the big one. A look at the record suggests, once more, that the true outcome is rather different. While a portion of social welfare spending in the form of food stamps, Medicaid and CETA job funds does get through to lower income people, most of it does not.

Consider: From 1965 to 1976 the amount of government money spent for "social welfare" functions broadly defined exploded from $77 billion a year to more than $331 billion—an increase of better than $250 billion in the amount of money being spent each year allegedly to help the needy. Interestingly, the number of poor people in America hardly changed at all during this period—continuing to hover at about the 25 million mark, according to the official figures (which overstate the problem by leaving out in-kind benefits).

A little arithmetic is sufficient to show that if we had taken this $250 billion increase in social welfare spending and simply given it to those 25 million poor people, we could have given each and every one of them an annual grant of $10,000—which is an income, for a family of four, of $40,000 a year. We could have made all those poor people relatively rich. But we didn't. So where is the money? The answer is that the bulk of it goes not to people who are poor but to up-scale citizens who have know-how, connections and leverage in the political process. Prominent among those receiving such funds are people who work in one fashion or another for government— teaching poor people, studying poor people or working in think tanks that ponder methods of helping poor people or administering government programs that allegedly render services to poor people.

It is these non-poor people who get about two thirds of the "social welfare" money and who are much better off—not only than poor people, but than the average taxpayers who foot the bills. In 1977, for example, the average income of a civilian employee of the federal government in the Washington, D.C., area was over $20,000 a year. The average income of taxpayers working in private industry was slightly over half of that—about $12,000. So to the extent that we increase funding for such programs, we are actually transferring money from people who are relatively poor—the taxpayers—to people who are relatively rich—people who work for, or with, the government.

In view of these comfortable pay scales, the findings of *Harper's* magazine a couple of years ago should hardly be surprising. In a piece entitled "The Wealth of Washington," this journal concluded that the nation's capital had become the richest community in the United States—with the highest per-household income in the nation. It's good to know that, in one community at least, the "war on poverty" has succeeded!

VII

*The Great American
Seed Corn Banquet*

The enemies of the Future are always the very
nicest people.

—Christopher Morley

As these words are written, advocates of a "no-growth" policy for the United States should be dancing in the streets. While their fellow citizens were minding their own business, the no-growthers saw their policies adopted. For most of the past decade, the American economy has hardly grown at all.

Any index you care to look at tells the story: Real Gross National Product has been inching forward at a snail's pace (an expansion of seven tenths of 1 percent is projected for the coming year); worker productivity per man-hour has fallen to less than a third of its former rate of increase and in 1979 declined; from 1973–79 there was *no* increase, to all intents and purposes, in output per worker employed in the U.S. economy; and between 1979 and 1980 the purchasing power of the average American family not only didn't grow—it shrank approximately 5 percent. Wonderful, isn't it?

While the no-growthers in their redwood hot-tubs may be toasting each other with Perrier over these developments, it is doubtful American workers and consumers generally will share in the enthusiasm. The decline in our rate of productivity advance has meant a loss of real income to American citizens—about $3700 less per family in 1978 than if the previous rate of growth (about 3 percent a year) had been permitted to continue.

If you could use an extra $4000 or so in annual purchasing power, then you are one of those who would benefit from economic growth. It is just such growth, historically, that has permitted Americans to enjoy an increasingly comfortable standard of living and to experience a level of economic satisfactions—including increased leisure for all kinds of discretionary activities—that far exceeds the attainments of its predecessors. Economist Ezra Solomon of Stanford states the issue—and the problem—this way:

"Over the past century, each American generation has enjoyed a standard of economic life *twice* as high as its parents—and we have come to accept this steady improvement as a fact of life. At the rate of improvement we have achieved since 1973 [however], it will take not one generation but 300 years to double average living standards. At the rate we have achieved over the past year, we will be lucky to maintain 1979 standards."

Why has our rate of economic growth and productivity been declining? There is no real mystery. Simply put, our nation is staggering under the tremendous weight of a government apparatus that absorbs almost

40 percent of GNP and distorts the workings of our economic process with its irrational policies. The combined effects of high tax rates, regulatory costs, government deficits and runaway inflation are causing our economy to grind down to zero. Add the explicit effort of certain elements in our society to *force* a no-growth policy on the nation and the outcome is a foregone conclusion.

We are back, again, to common sense. It is impossible to consume what is not produced. And to produce something, you must have three elements: incentive, means and access to resources. The incentive is whatever it is that makes people work to better their condition. The means are the tools with which they are provided. The resources consist of the natural abundance of the earth, including soil, timber, mineral deposits, energy supplies.

It is from this combination of factors that all economic progress from the dawn of time has occurred—from the agricultural revolution to the industrial revolution to the recent success stories of Japan, West Germany and Taiwan. Wherever people have the incentive to work and improve their condition, the tools with which to do it and the resources with which to get the job done, they have been able to increase their productivity, creating more and better goods with the same—or measured in terms of muscle power—less human effort.

What has happened in the United States in recent years is that we have effectively neutralized *all* these preconditions to economic growth—taking away the incentive and the means to greater productivity and systematically closing off access to the required resources. In so doing, we have not only locked the average American into a stagnant or declining standard of living, we have helped ensure that people mired in poverty have no reasonable chance of getting out of it. For a political creed that glories in its supposed compassion for the downtrodden, this would seem to be an anomalous outcome.

Such problems are usually discussed in dry economic terms, and some comprehension of economics is useful in understanding all the implications of what we have been doing to ourselves. But the basic problem is not economic—it is moral and intellectual. It is rooted in the moral failure that has afflicted our nation in recent years. This, after all, is the "now" generation which wants to make it through the night and let the devil take tomorrow. Nowhere is this mentality more obvious than in our national economic policies. Our productivity troubles are simply one aspect of a national passion for living for the moment, refusing to make provision for the future—what I call "the great American seed corn banquet."

For any nation that wants to maintain its strength and provide a rising standard of living for its people, the "seed corn" is that portion of its resources it sets aside for growth and development. It represents a decision to forego *present consumption* in order to provide for *future benefits*. It can consist of, literally, seed corn, or time taken to construct a better fishing pole, or a hoe, or buying a tractor, investment in industrial equipment, computers or satellite technology. It is that portion of present earnings set aside to provide for better and more effective tools that will enhance productivity. In our economy, the "seed corn" is the amount of resources we devote to better equipment, research and development, and technological and other innovations that permit continued forward movement along the path of economic progress. Such investment in the future in a vast society such as our own requires staggering set-asides—according to one estimate, better than $4 trillion in the period 1974–85 to finance the capital needs of our economy. The amount of money is huge, but it takes only a small downward shift in the growth of our economy to deprive us of its benefits.

Investment on this scale is needed, in the first place, to provide new jobs for our expanding work force. For a variety of reasons above and beyond natural population increase, our labor force has grown enormously in recent years. In the past decade alone, some 18 million new jobs have been provided for American workers. Since it takes more than $40,000 to provide a single job in American industry, the demand for investment capital to handle this continued influx into the economy is obvious. To provide employment for all these people and enhance the living standards of American society generally will require an enormous investment of "seed corn."

If you eat the seed corn, however, you can't plant it. To the degree that we divert resources from savings and investment to the heedless pleasures of immediate consumption, we decrease our harvest. This is exactly what we have been doing in America in recent years.

In May of 1975 I went before the Senate Finance Committee on one of my numerous treks to Capitol Hill to plead for savings, investment and productivity and to warn against the dangers of what we were doing to our economy. I spelled out the record that showed us lagging behind other nations in terms of providing for the economic future, discussed the negative impact of taxes, inflation and regulatory costs and deplored the adverse effects that all of this would have on the health of our economy and the standard of living of our citizens. I regret to say that in the five years since this sermon was delivered, nothing has happened to change its bleak prognosis.

Over the past two decades, the United States has brought up the rear among industrial nations in percentage of Gross National Product held as personal savings. From 1973–77 other industrial nations were saving between 10 percent (Canada) and 25 percent (Japan) of GNP. During that same span, the United States saved only 6.7 percent, and in the past year the savings rate has fallen as low as 3.4 percent.

All investment comes directly or indirectly out of somebody's savings—either private or business—and U.S. investment rates have predictably declined with the fall-off of personal savings. In the period 1962–78 the United States ranked dead last among eight major industrial nations in average investment as a percentage of GNP. Our average rate was 17.5 percent, barely more than *half* the Japanese rate of 32 percent. Unsurprisingly, in view of this much higher investment rate, the Japanese have three times our rate of productivity increase and a 137 percent higher rate of growth for GNP.

The results of this shortfall in U.S. savings and investment are intensely practical for those who want to get better jobs—or hold the ones they have. Because other countries have been surging ahead of us in savings and investment, they have also been outproducing us in many industries. This means their products are bought in other countries in place of our own—and, in many instances, in the United States as well. Electronics, textiles, steel and automobiles are examples of industries in which we have fallen behind in terms of technological advance and productivity. This loss of global markets means loss of

jobs. *Business Week* estimates that the resulting decline in U.S. economic power meant $125 billion in
lost production in the 1970s and the loss of two million plus jobs in the American economy.

While some people like to treat this decline in
savings, investment and productivity as a deep mystery, it is about as mysterious as the fact that rain
causes wet sidewalks. If we had sat down and listed
everything a nation could possibly do to discourage
investment in the future, while accentuating present-
oriented consumption, the list would not look very
different from the policies we have been following.
The federal government has catered our seed corn
banquet with exquisite attention to detail, leaving
nothing undone that might prevent effective planning
for the future.

In this respect, of course, the caterer is superbly
qualified. Politics is a profession in which the time
horizons are notoriously short, long-term perspectives
conspicuous by their absence. The typical "compassionate" politician is not concerned about such boring
stuff as accumulating capital for the next generation;
he is much more interested in accumulating votes for
the next election. And historically, this short-term
goal has been accomplished by promising handouts
to all and sundry—paying for present consumption
with taxes and inflation that eat away at capital.

The same nose-length perspective marks the do-it-
now regulators who demand instant solutions to what
they see as problems—and never mind the costs. This
mentality has loaded huge regulatory expenses on our
business system (costs which are promptly passed on
to the consumer) and diverted a tremendous percentage of corporate research and development to compliance with government standards rather than seeking

ways to greater productivity. In these go-go regulatory circles, distinguished by a total lack of knowledge of the business world, there seems to be a belief that American industry can do anything if it is simply ordered to do it. This naive faith in the wonder-working powers of business would be quite touching if it were not so obviously steeped in malice.

Finally, politics is a profession in which the *appearance* of doing something of alleged benefit to the public (before the next election) is far more important than the *substance* of doing something. It was for this reason, for example, that President Nixon put wage and price controls into effect in 1971—even though he knew they would be ineffective, and worse, as a method of combatting inflation. The motive was political—to quiet the political clamor in Congress to "do something" visible about rising prices. This factor is an added motivation for slapping on controls or adopting other measures purely for short-term effect, regardless of the long-term consequences.

With all that going for it, we should not be surprised that the federal government as currently operated has devised a comprehensive program for devouring economic seed corn as fast as it can be shoveled from the granary. The first and most obvious problem is simply the amount of resources that our enormous government consumes directly. The 40 percent plus of GNP being gobbled up by government at all levels is 40 percent plus of GNP that, by definition, is not available for private savings and investment. This government spending is almost entirely devoted to current consumption at the expense of long-term future planning.

It is true that some of the dollars spent by governments on such projects as energy research or building pyramids are *called* investment, and there are examples of government outlay that have long-term productive consequences (atomic energy is an example, the space program another). But for the most part, government spending projects simply represent dollars that are diverted from the task of improving industrial plants or providing needed technological innovation. The same is true of the $120 billion in mandated regulatory costs imposed on industry—and consumers. These dollars may "create jobs" for pollution controllers, OSHA inspectors, safety consultants and manufacturers of catalytic converters, but they do not add to the productive potential of the nation or contribute to the economic standard of living of the average American.

As Professor Paul MacAvoy of Yale puts it: ". . . the reallocation of investment from productivity-increasing projects to regulation probably reduces overall GNP growth by one quarter to one half a percentage point a year alone. If you take this half percent a year of foregone productivity growth over a decade, you're going to find the economy essentially running six or seven percent below its capacity potential because of these controls alone. Regulation has thus spread widely and effectively to encompass about a third of our output and has thereby reduced our productivity growth significantly."

In addition to these general features of federal policy, there are aspects of what our government is doing that seem specifically designed to discourage business and private savings and consequent investment. Profits are taxed up to 46 percent. Dividends are taxed twice, first at the corporate level, then at the personal level,* economic gains from holding stocks are diminished through "capital gains" taxes, interest on savings accounts is taxed as "unearned" personal income. All of these are levies against the future-oriented process of savings and investment used to finance the continued orgy of political consumption described in Chapter III.

Indirect effects of this onerous tax system further divert resources from future-oriented, productive investment. The search for tax shelters, such as real estate and municipal bonds, or inflation hedges, such as gold or art objects, diverts funds from the normal flow of productive investment. An enormous amount of time and energy is spent on devising methods to cushion the effect of taxes—time and energy that cannot be devoted to productive effort. One aspect of this development is the growth of a huge "underground" economy consisting of cash transactions where there is no record of the exchange or barter in which services are exchanged directly. While these activities if computed would actually increase our GNP, the time and effort involved in arranging them are great, and the process is incredibly inefficient compared to more usual financial arrangements. Some months ago, the IRS estimated that $184 billion a year in income (a sum almost as large as the GNP of Canada) goes unreported in the United States. Peter Gutmann of City University of New York has put the figure at $220 billion a year, while economist Edgar Feige of the University of Wisconsin says it's $540 billion—more than a quarter of our officially tabulated GNP.

The effects of direct taxation on savings, invest-

* It should be noted, of course, that corporations don't pay taxes, consumers do.

ment and productivity are almost trivial, however, compared to the effects of inflation. Chronic inflation, borrowing against the future to finance the political pleasures of the hour, is more than a seed corn banquet—it is a Roman orgy. The ways in which it destroys capital, discourages savings and investment and decreases productivity are almost too numerous to elaborate. Suffice it to say that if one really wanted a "no-growth" posture for America, the policy of deficits and inflation we have pursued in recent years is enough, all by itself, to get the job done. A few examples:

—When the federal government goes into the money markets to finance its huge deficits, it sops up capital that cannot be used by private business. In recent years this "crowding out" effect has gone as high as 35 to 40 percent of total borrowing in the economy. This pushes up the rate of interest and, as noted, leads to expansionary policies to make sufficient credit available for other borrowers—i.e., creation of new money, or inflation.

—By its very nature, inflation is calculated to discourage savings and investment and to encourage present consumption and debt. If the purchasing power of the dollar is going to be cut in half in a decade, it makes little sense for me to hold that dollar in a savings account. Better to spend it now while it still has some purchasing power left. In fact, it pays me to consume not only everything I have but also what I *don't* have—in other words, go into debt. I can pay back my creditors in the future with dollars that are worth less than the ones I borrow.

—The undesirability of savings is accentuated by the fact that federal tax policies impose a tax on the nominal rate of interest while making no allowance for inflation. If the true rate of interest is 4 percent and the inflation rate is 12 percent, the interest you receive as a saver/lender would be 16 percent. If you are in a 50 percent marginal tax bracket, you would pay 8 percent of this in taxes. With your remaining 8 percent profit pitted against the 12 percent inflation rate, you would be the loser by 4 percentage points.

—Even this rate of return, however, has been available only to large savers. If you are a small saver with a passbook account, as noted, the situation is much worse. Just to make sure that small savers lose badly under present inflationary conditions, the federal government imposed a rule (Regulation Q) which limited interest on passbook accounts to just over 5 percent. At a 13 percent inflation rate, this means an 8 percent loss on your money. If you are in the 30 percent tax bracket, 5 percent interest after taxes is 3.5 percent, meaning your loss is 9.5 percent. The annual loss to savers from this ridiculous provision (whose abolition I repeatedly urged when I was at Treasury) has been estimated at $75 billion. Naturally, as small savers got wise to this ripoff, they started withdrawing money from such accounts.

—Similar considerations apply to business in its effort to get and retain earnings for investment or to attract equity capital. Tax writeoffs for depreciation become grossly unrealistic under inflationary conditions since replacement costs are so much higher than the historical cost of acquisition. Profits and resulting taxes are correspondingly overstated, while taxes imposed on capital gains—even at the reduced rate of the 1978 reform—are taxes on inflationary increases and thus amount to a confiscation of capital. (We are one of the few countries in the world even to have such a tax.)

While there have been managerial lapses in some industries, businessmen in general are concerned about future investment. They have to be; unless they make provision for plant improvements and new equipment, they will go out of business. The rate of business savings in our economy has therefore remained relatively constant through the years—despite the inflation and other governmental obstacles—at slightly under 12 percent of GNP. However, so much of this has to be diverted to meet government regulatory requirements and satisfy the demand for inflation-hedging purchases by the public (especially residential housing) that the total amount invested in new and better equipment has been pathetically meager. Professor Michael Boskin estimates that in 1979 real net addition to plant and equipment actually amounted to less than 2 percent of GNP. This works out to approximately $40 billion or roughly *one third* of the amount that business had to invest to comply with governmental regulations.

The decline of private savings has been further accentuated by government policies telling people they don't *need* to worry about the future. Historically, people have saved to improve their living standards and provide for themselves in emergencies, illness or retirement. If government is going to do all these things for you, why do it for yourself? The prime example is Social Security, which has assumed a large part of the place once occupied in future planning by personal thrift. The difference is that Social Security consists of transfer payments financed from present earnings, while the equivalent arrangement through private savings or pensions would make funds available for investment. Harvard's Martin Feldstein has estimated the net result has been to divert as much as $61 billion a year from private savings.*

Finally, recall our discussion concerning the "bracket creep" effect of inflation, pushing people into constantly higher tax brackets and lowering real income. The constantly climbing tax rates imposed by this process are a positive disincentive to put forth extra effort—and while an incentive component is hard to quantify, any employer can tell you it is a major factor in running a successful, productive business. At the same time that we have discouraged energetic productive work, we have deployed vast incentives in favor of not working at all: welfare payments, unemployment compensation, food stamps and the rest of it—the very programs we are financing with our runaway system of taxes and inflation.

As noted, transfer payments from people who are working to people who are not working now amount to 53 percent of our gargantuan federal budget. This is a machine for penalizing work and rewarding idleness. Since 1969, wages and salaries in the United States have grown at an average annual rate of 9.1 percent—while transfer payments were growing at an annual rate of 14.3 percent. In other words, we have been increasing rewards for *not* working at a much more rapid pace than the increase in compensation for productive labor. The result is that what little gain

---

* Social Security, it should be added, is a prize example of a government program that started on one premise and wound up on another. When the system was launched, it was supposed to be a pay-as-you-go insurance program, supplementing retirement income at a nominal cost of $30 a year in taxes per person. Today it is a mammoth welfare program disbursing over $100 billion annually, with terrible long-term actuarial problems and a tax burden so huge that, for a majority of U.S. families, it is the largest single tax they pay.

there has been in economic productivity in recent years has gone to recipients of transfer payments rather than to the working taxpayer.

If all of this seems more than sufficient to pulverize all hope of improving U.S. productivity, rest assured that there is more. So far, I have been discussing only the first two elements of productivity growth—means and incentive. The third is access to resources—meaning raw materials, minerals, energy supplies, etc. And here too, we discover, the federal planners have been hard at work to make certain that we lack the wherewithal to maintain or upgrade our economy. In fact, the horror story on this front is so incredibly bad that it deserves comparison with the Gothic lunacy we call inflation.

VIII

Shutting Down the Dynamo

Any nation that can put a man on the moon
should be able to abolish the Department of
Energy.

—ANONYMOUS

Some caustic—and accurate—critic of the Soviet system once said that if the communists ever got control
of the Sahara Desert, they would soon create a shortage of sand.

Shortages are built into collectivist systems. Under
political decision-making that prevents the orderly
operation of markets and crushes incentives to production, shortages are a way of life. Prior to the Bol-
shevik revolution, Russia was a major exporter of
wheat. Since the takeover, it has been chronically
unable to feed its people—and has to import food-
stuffs (and a great deal else) from the capitalist West,
especially the United States.

While shortages are inevitable under collectivist

planning, the planners seldom admit they are to blame. It is always the fault of someone else—greedy peasants, evil landlords, consumers who demand too much. A favorite explanation of bad harvests in the Soviet Union is weather. Apparently, there has been bad growing weather in Russia in almost every year since 1917.

Similar effects—and similar alibis—are surfacing now in the United States. As our productive power falters and economic standards tumble under the weight of excess government, the political planners who have created the mess blame anyone or anything except themselves. The clearest example is the case of energy, where we have been wrestling with problems of falling production, continuing shortages, painful gas lines and other economic dislocations.

The most popular "analysis" of our energy troubles, promoted by the "no-growth" faction, the Club of Rome and spokesmen for the Carter Administration, is that we are simply running out of energy—especially oil and natural gas. In this scenario, we are like the greedy peasants of the Soviet Union: We have been "energy pigs," gobbling up resources, living in overheated houses, driving in high-powered cars. Now, the Carter Administration tells us, we are running up against the natural limits and must learn to do without—park our cars, turn down our thermostats and pull on our cardigan sweaters.

All of which is unadulterated nonsense. Projections of natural exhaustion of our petroleum reserves have been heard repeatedly in the past—and they have always been mistaken. In 1914 the Bureau of Mines said our petroleum supplies were severely limited, and in 1919 the director of the bureau said the end of the petroleum era was in sight. Similar official statements were heard in 1926, 1939 and 1949—all of them completely wrong.

The reason such projections were mistaken—and are mistaken now—is that they failed to grasp the workings of a free economy. What has always happened in the past is that as demand for oil increased, putting upward pressure on prices, producers went out to obtain and market more of it. The market pricing mechanism brought supply and demand into harmony, increasing output in tempo with consumption.

That mechanism has been unable to work in recent years, however, because the federal government won't let it. Controls on the wellhead price of petroleum and the pump price of gasoline were imposed in 1971 as part of the Nixon program of wage and price controls and were kept there in 1973 even when they were lifted on everything else. Prior to the imposition of controls, our proved reserves of crude oil, with occasional variations, had continually increased— from 20 billion barrels in 1945 to almost 40 billion in 1970. Since the controls went into effect, our proved reserves have consistently fallen.

Incredible as it may seem, we were actually producing less oil in the United States at the end of the 1970s than we had been at the beginning—despite the steady upward pressure of demand. In fact, by holding prices artificially low, the controls encouraged consumption even further. And if you produce less of something while consuming more of it, you end up with a shortage. As a result, despite much talk of "energy independence," our imports of petroleum moved up from approximately 35 percent of our consumption needs in 1973 to 43 percent in 1978 to over 50 percent in 1980.

All of this is lost on bureaucratic Chicken Littles,

who keep telling us the energy sky has fallen in for natural reasons. In fact, the potential energy resources of the United States—including oil, natural gas, coal and nuclear—remain incredibly vast and are nowhere near depletion. There are tens of billions of barrels of oil still waiting to be discovered and produced in the United States, 600 billion barrels of shale oil, untold trillions of cubic feet of natural gas, an 800-year supply of coal and a virtually limitless energy resource in nuclear power.

An excellent study sponsored by the Ford Foundation, entitled *Energy: The Next Twenty Years,* sums up the situation this way:

"The potential energy resources of the United States and the world are so large that the ultimate physical exhaustion of energy in general is hardly a matter for present concern—with proper policy and planning and a willingness to pay the costs, energy can be produced to meet any reasonable projection of demand, without 'gaps' or physical shortages."

The "energy shortage," in other words, is a creation of the federal government. Price controls are only a part of it. The government has taken numerous other steps to close off petroleum production while increasing consumption, including refusal to lease offshore lands for drilling, imposition of environmental standards that prevent construction of refineries, mandated emission and safety features on automobiles that require greater oil consumption, etc.

Ralph Kinney Bennett of *Reader's Digest* lists the myriad bureaucratic controls that prevent the production and use of petroleum: taxes on domestic production (to subsidize imports), 250 different forms from the Department of Energy that have to be filled out a total of 940,000 times a year, environmentalist delays on drilling projects and numerous other types of interference including the withholding of federal lands from exploration.

The most glaring example of this last-named policy is the battle that has been waged over Alaska—which Eastern "environmentalists" are fighting to keep as a perpetual wilderness. The benefits of Prudhoe Bay were held up for six years by environmental squabbling over the Alaska pipeline, until Congress finally passed a special law to push it through. Prudhoe Bay was the largest single oil strike ever made in the United States—but some experts estimate it is barely the tip of the Alaskan iceberg.

Alaska covers 566,000 square miles, of which Prudhoe Bay accounts for only 400. The vast interior of the state has hardly been explored at all. Only seven oil rigs are currently working in the state (compared to 366 in Louisiana and 807 in Texas). When we consider that Prudhoe Bay alone has ten billion barrels of proved reserves, the potential of Alaska is colossal—estimated at anywhere from 49 billion to 200 billion barrels.

The no-growthers and counterculture advocates in the Carter Administration, however, have fought like men possessed to close Alaska off from energy development. The Carter Administration has been fighting to put 140 million acres of the state—about 40 percent of the total land area—into a federal deep freeze as a "national monument." So committed was the Administration to this scheme that when Congress refused to pass the bill it wanted in 1978, the President and his Secretary of Interior, invoking other provisions of the law, ordered the lockup on their own. If they have their way, Alaska's energy potential will never be realized.

What has been happening in Alaska is symbolic of what has been happening to our Western lands in general—lands that contain a huge potential not only for energy supplies but other mineral resources. Great chunks of these Western states are owned by the federal government—Alaska, 96 percent, Nevada, 86 percent, Utah, 65 percent, Idaho, 64 percent, and so on. It has been estimated that 85 percent of the nation's oil reserves are located on federal land. But restrictionist policies have been such that two thirds of the publicly owned land in the United States is now foreclosed from petroleum exploration.

All of this, mind you, concerns only the regulatory snafu that surrounds *petroleum*. A similar sad story could be told of natural gas, which has been subject to interstate price controls since the middle 1950s, resulting in the usual shortages as consumption rose and production for the national market fell. In the intrastate markets of producing states like Texas, where federal price controls did not apply, there was no shortage. Looking at the discrepancy, the energy planners in the Carter Administration and the Congress knew exactly what had to be done: They extended controls into the intrastate market!

This dismal litany goes on and on—to environmental standards that restrict the mining and burning of coal, rules that forced conversion from coal to oil (and government edicts to compel conversion back again), emission standards that demanded greater fuel consumption and, of course, the clamorous battle to halt production of nuclear power. The totality of the problem becomes apparent. *There is no aspect of our energy economy today that is not wrapped up tightly in a stifling cocoon of government red tape.*

The "problem" the federal government proposes

to solve with its $11 billion Department of Energy, Niagara of "studies" and pilot projects and endless thousands of regulations is thus entirely the doing of the federal government itself. And of course, the taxes required to pay for all this extra governing and the controls imposed by all the regulations only serve to make the problem worse. Having noticed that the energy boat is sinking, the federal regulators propose to bore some more holes in the boat to let the water out. (This is typical of the bureaucratic mentality.)

It is worth observing, as an added comment on this subject, that massive government interference with our energy supplies has not attained the goals projected for it *even in terms of lower price*. Because we have choked off our own production, we have made ourselves increasingly dependent on OPEC and thus required to pay its prices. The net effect of regulation is thus to make our petroleum costs much higher— by as much as $3 billion, according to the recent Ford Foundation–sponsored study.

Again, consider the irony of an allegedly "liberal" and "compassionate" policy of top-down government regulation—a policy that has anything but humane results. Looking at such policies across the board, we may well inquire what is so "compassionate" about a government that drives up energy (and other) costs to the consumer, destroys the productive power of our economy, brings a halt to economic growth that alone can lift the poor from their condition, imposes stifling taxes and regulations that dominate our lives, and eats up the pensions and savings of the elderly with double-digit, runaway inflation.

The energy issue is crucial to our survival and to our hopes for restoring America's economic vigor. There is a close correlation between per capita energy use and the economic attainments of a nation in terms of industrial progress and standard of living for the average citizen. Which stands to reason, since energy is the capacity to do work. It is the lifeblood of an economic system; choke off the supply of energy, and the heart of the economy will falter and ultimately shudder to a stop.

It is this central fact that makes our present energy policies so appalling. As with other regulatory failures, much of government's negative impact on energy production can be considered accidental—the byproduct of thoughtless interference aiming at short-term popular goals like low petroleum prices, without sufficient understanding of how the economic process operates. In this respect, energy is like many other industries, staggering beneath a massive burden of taxes, inflation and controls.

The situation in energy is *worse*, however, because it has been so plainly targeted for special agitation. It is no accident that the Fonda-Nader-Commoner axis, the environmentalists and the no-growth counterculture spend so much time denouncing oil companies, opposing nuclear power and otherwise blasting the existing system of energy production in this country. To many people this might seem merely curious or coincidental, but it has an obvious logic: If you want to bring about the "de-industrialization" of the United States, shutting off its supply of energy is the most certain way to do it.

Gauging the mix of motives between sheer bureaucratic stupidity and deliberate efforts to force us into energy starvation is difficult, and unnecessary. Suffice it to say the effort to shut down our energy supplies has been so complete, and stifling, that the net effect is indistinguishable from the counterculture program. Federal energy policies are like a tourniquet around our nation's windpipe. What we confront, through ignorance or through design, is a campaign to throttle every conceivable energy supply from currently available sources.

All of this, as noted, is directly in keeping with the Lovins-Schumacher push for "soft and small" in energy production—wind and solar power, or maybe fuzzy rabbits on a treadmill. Such cream-puff notions may or may not be adequate for small-scale personal use, but there is no way that we can run our vast industrial economy on such a basis. Which means, if the recent trend continues, that we can no longer have mass-production industries, enjoy the standard of living to which Americans have been accustomed or be a major power in the world arena. It is hard to envision a solar-powered submarine or a supersonic bomber propelled by windmills, and equally hard to envision an America that can play a leading role in international dealings if it is piddling around with backyard energy schemes at home.

This prospect, of course, disturbs the soft-and-smallers not at all. In fact, an abdication of American prestige and power in the world is a key objective of the counterculture, as shall be noted in the following chapter. De-industrialization of America in domestic economics goes hand in glove with American withdrawal and retreat in foreign affairs.

In the aftermath of World War II, a policy was devised within the American government for converting Nazi Germany into a purely agricultural society. It was called the "Morgenthau" plan, after one of my predecessors at the Treasury Department. The idea was to flatten Germany as an industrial power—to remove its industrial base and to compel its citizens to revert to a bucolic life, on the principle that any nation deprived of its industrial might could never be a major military factor in the world.

The Morgenthau plan for Germany was rejected, on the grounds that such a scheme was inhumane. Because it was rejected, and because West Germany under Ludwig Erhard threw off the burden of postwar controls and moved toward a free economy, Germany became a strong industrial nation once again. And that development was fortunate since Germany today is not only strong and peaceful but stands as a major barrier to Soviet ambitions in Western Europe.

History, however, can take ironic twists: While we failed to impose the Morgenthau plan on Germany, we are now engaged, it seems, in imposing it on ourselves. The combination of our energy shutdown, massive government taxes and controls, the decline in productivity and economic growth, the collapse of major U.S. industries and the explicit advocacy of the counterculture all point in one direction—a brave new world of impotence for the United States.

IX

The Trumpet That Always Sounds Retreat

We often give our enemies the means of our destruction.

—AESOP'S FABLES

If anything should be more frightening to American citizens than our domestic weaknesses, it is the drastic deterioration of our defenses and the concomitant collapse of our position abroad. This problem is so serious that our economic troubles should seem paltry by comparison—if only because the demise of America as a free and independent nation would make all our internal troubles meaningless.

In fact, however, the problems are closely intertwined. As noted, weakness on the home front begets weakness overseas, and both forms of national feebleness are rooted in a common set of moral and intellectual failings. The same kind of defeatist psychology is at work, spread by the same kind of people, aiming at much the same objectives. Even the methods used to induce our global weakness are the same as those employed in our domestic politics.

That the United States has lost colossal chunks of ground to the Soviet Union in terms of strategic preparedness is at this point conceded by just about everyone—including spokesmen for the Carter Administration. From a position of clear strategic superiority in the middle 1960s, we have slipped to a point where the Soviets outnumber us in strategic missiles, submarine-launched missiles, tanks, combat planes, naval vessels and most other indicators of military prowess.

Virtually the only category where we technically still have a lead is in long-range bombers (where we led the Soviets 1300 to 170 in 1964 and now lead 348 to 156)—and this figure is inflated since our superior numbers derive from our inventory of aged B-52s, a plane designed before the Korean War. As General Daniel Graham observes, going into battle now with the B-52 would be the equivalent of going into World War II with Spads and Sopwith Camels.

Perhaps the most incredible imbalance between the United States and the Soviet Union is in the realm of strategic defenses against air or missile attack. As of 1978, the Soviets had deployed more than 12,000 defensive missiles to knock down incoming aircraft or projectiles and had 2700 interceptor aircraft. We had 990 SAM launchers and 108 active fighter aircraft (with another 162 in the National Guard)—putting us in the minus category by roughly 14,000 weapons.

Most of this strategic transformation has occurred because the United States has been standing still or going backwards. Our continued reliance on the B-52 and our huge imbalance in air defense are but two examples. Naval power is yet another, as our number of carriers was cut in half in the decade of the '70s, and 94 destroyers were decommissioned and only four were added. While the Soviets have continued surging forward, we have been sliding into military impotence.

The Soviet lead in ICBMs and submarine-launched missiles, combined with our almost total absence of strategic defenses, means that Moscow would have a good chance of knocking out many of our offensive weapons and surviving any counterpunch we might decide to throw. In fact, a careful study done for Rep. Robin Beard of Tennessee indicated that "even with proposed force modernization programs, the U.S. from now until 1984 would be militarily better off not retaliating after a Soviet counterforce attack" since any retaliation on our part would simply invite another punishing bombardment.

Contrary to the idea that strategic superiority is meaningless in the modern world, the Soviets have used their growing military edge to flex their muscles and extend their influence in every quarter of the globe. The invasion of Afghanistan and the presence of 3000 Soviet combat troops in Cuba are among the more visible manifestations of this boldness but far from isolated.

Look at virtually any trouble spot in the world today and you find the influence of the Soviets and their Cuban and East German stooges. An estimated 50,000 Cuban troops are deployed in Africa and, together with Soviet ordnance and East German "advisers," have helped establish Marxist beachheads in Angola, Mozambique and Ethiopia, have assisted in bringing to power a Marxist regime in Zimbabwe-Rhodesia whose ultimate direction is yet to be decided and are focusing increased pressures on mineral-rich

Zaire, Namibia and South Africa.

In Asia, all of Vietnam is now subjected to the rule of Soviet-sponsored communists in Hanoi who have overrun the neighboring despotism in Cambodia and, as these words are written, are staging incursions across the border into Thailand. Laos also has come under communist domination, and the hard-line Stalinists in North Korea continue to menace their anti-communist neighbor to the south. The dominoes that weren't supposed to exist in Asia are toppling rapidly in the Soviets' direction.

In the oil-rich Persian Gulf region, the Shah of Iran has, of course, been replaced by a fanatic regime which is heavily influenced by the Marxist Tudeh Party and has been engaging in a reign of terror including the kidnapping of more than 50 American hostages. Afghanistan has been subjugated by Soviet troops. South Yemen is ruled by a Soviet puppet regime. Anti-communist Muslim states such as Saudi Arabia express alarm at the virtually unimpeded advance of Soviet power in the area.

In Latin America, Cuba itself is, of course, a model communist fiefdom. Small nations such as Grenada have fallen under Castroite domination. Panama's Torrijos is closely aligned with Castro, as are the Sandinistas of Nicaragua—who have journeyed to Moscow to express their solidarity with the Soviets, including support for the invasion of Afghanistan. Marxist forces backed by Castro and Nicaragua are currently battering away at El Salvador and Guatemala.

While all this is going on, where is the United States? As the Soviets and Cubans worked their will in Africa, our former ambassador to the United Nations, Andrew Young, declared the Cubans were a

"stabilizing" force, voiced his friendship for the
Marxist rulers of Mozambique and joined in undermining a democratically elected black anti-communist
government in Zimbabwe-Rhodesia. After having
claimed the Shah of Iran as a stalwart friend, the
Carter Administration abandoned him in his hour of
need. Far from helping fend off the Marxist takeover
of Nicaragua, the U.S. State Department assisted the
Sandinistas into power.

While the Soviets and their allies inexorably advance, the U.S. government displays a profile of fu-
tility and impotence. Our response to the invasion of
Afghanistan was to boycott the Olympics and declare
an embargo on *extra* grain shipments to the U.S.S.R.—
while, behind the scenes, the flow of U.S. technology
to the Soviets was scarcely interrupted. Our answer
to the Iranian kidnapping of our citizens was a pathetic
rescue operation in which our helicopters malfunc-
tioned and crashed and U.S. servicemen died in
flames—and no hostages were rescued. When Soviet
combat troops were discovered in Cuba, we issued
a virtual ultimatum to the Kremlin—and then with-
drew it.

Our tail-between-the-legs retreat has not only encouraged the Soviets to audacity but invited the in-
solence of mobs and revolutionaries around the world.
American citizens and representatives of our government are considered fair game for any terrorist, and
data from the State Department and the CIA indicate
that, in the past decade, more than 600 American
personnel overseas have been subject to attack. Our
embassies are sacked and burned, our ambassadors
kidnaped and murdered, our flag reviled and trampled
on. Similar attacks on Soviet and East European personnel, meantime, are almost nonexistent.

The meaning of these events is not lost on other nations. Watching the Soviet advance and U.S. retreat and observing the fate of those in Vietnam, Iran and Nicaragua who counted on American support, our remaining allies are gravely worried about what will happen to them unless they come to terms with Moscow. In the wake of the Afghan invasion, Pakistan turned down suggested U.S. arms aid and switched its most influential ambassador from Washington to Moscow. West Germany, which stands athwart the path of any Soviet invasion of Western Europe, is known to be weighing the merits of a separate settlement. Similar thoughts are bruited about in the Middle East. The continuing spectacle of our impotence and unreliability, as the *Wall Street Journal* puts it, "is having no small effect on world politics."

For a nation that was once the most powerful in the world and which despite its troubles still has the potential of being so again, this is an incredible scenario. In a relatively brief span of years, the United States has fallen from a position of global power and eminence to second spot in most categories of military strength, watched in helpless agony as its citizens have been taken captive and stood by idly as one country after another has been drawn into the Marxist vortex. We live in a world today where it is far more dangerous to be America's friend than it is to be her enemy, and our government proposes nothing that could make the situation better.

Like our weakness on the home front, this erosion of American power and prestige is largely self-inflicted. To be more precise, it is deliberate policy. The truth of the matter, incredible as it may seem, is that foreign policy theoreticians in and around the Carter State Department have consciously set out to pull back our defenses, renounce the use of American power in the world, assist Marxist revolutionary movements in toppling anti-communist governments and help build up the economic and military muscle of the Soviets.

That such deliberate weakening of our defenses, renunciation of our power and abandonment of our allies could actually be the official policy of the United States seems almost beyond belief. Certainly the average American would be stunned and outraged if he knew that such a thing were happening. But, as on the domestic front, what is told the average citizen and what is actually done in the realm of policy are miles apart. The strategy we are pursuing proceeds, again, from intellectual theorists of the counterculture and has been fastened into place without debate and in concealment from the American people.

Symbolic of the counterculture perspective on foreign policy—the functional equivalent of the Fonda-Nader-Commoner axis on the home front—is something called the Institute for Policy Studies. This radical Washington-based group professes a world view that says the United States and its allies are responsible for the Cold War and other evils in the world, seeks to overthrow anti-communist governments in favor of Marxist revolutionaries, battles to cut back U.S. defense spending and scuttle its intelligence agencies and in general tries to dismantle America's power in the world. The IPS viewpoint was summarized in a recent issue of *Barron's*:

"In Congress . . . IPS has concentrated its efforts on undermining support for the defense budget (in the name of 'human needs'), making it impossible for the intelligence agencies to function (in the name of 'freedom of speech') and denying the legitimacy of governments allied with or friendly to the United States (in the name of 'human rights'). Since the ability of the United States to maintain itself as a great power rests on its defense forces, its intelligence services and its allies, IPS has concentrated upon the crucial areas in its campaign to destroy the United States as what IPS calls 'the violence colony.'"*

As with the Fonda-Nader-Commoner axis, the views and activities of the IPS would seem to be so far out that they couldn't possibly have anything to do with the actual workings of American policy. Yet by dint of constant agitation, highly favorable exposure in the media and excellent entree into the councils of the Carter Administration, the IPS perspective on the world and many of its specific policy proposals have been converted into official strategy.** Matching them up point for point, it is hard to find any major initiative proposed by IPS that the Carter Administration has not adopted.

The degree to which the IPS agenda for American abdication has been converted into national policy has been spelled out by Carl Gershman, vice chairman of the Social Democrats U.S.A., in *Commentary* magazine. Gershman traces the rise of what he calls the "new foreign policy establishment" in the United States, describes their policy views (and linkages to IPS) and shows the method by which they have assumed the crucial policy-making roles within the Carter Administration. Among those discussed in this

---

*A major project of IPS is the presentation of its "alternate budget"—which proposes financing more domestic handouts by cutting back on expenditures for defense.

**The article in *Barron's* points out that, in a span of four months, the New York *Times* featured no less than nine essays by IPSers—without revealing the radical nature of the organization.

connection are Richard Holbrooke, Leslie Gelb, Paul Warnke, Anthony Lake and Richard Moose—all appointed to key positions by Jimmy Carter.

The common theme of the "new establishment" is the belief that anti-communism is passé and that we should forget such obsolete notions as contesting the Soviets, building up our strategic arsenal or supporting anti-communist states beset by Marxist insurrection or invasion. In the view of the "new establishment," as Gershman puts it, the key idea has been that "the containment of communism by the United States was neither possible nor necessary, nor even desirable."

In this perspective, the Cold War is the fault of the United States. Moscow's arms buildup and other aggressive behavior are allegedly a defensive response to our own. Also, according to this view, we have placed ourselves on the wrong side of history by opposing the "forces of change" in the undeveloped world. The indicated recourse is to phase down our arms commitment and stop being "provocative" to the Kremlin and to quit shoring up anti-communist regimes in contested areas around the world.

Because explicit political statements about such subjects are usually cautious, Mr. Carter and his advisers have not spelled this view of things out in quite so blunt a fashion to the American people. But the rhetorical signals and the actions of this Administration have made it crystal clear that, so far as our present policy-makers are concerned, the Cold War is over and done with and that, as Carter put it in a famous speech at Notre Dame, our strategy will no longer be guided by "an inordinate fear of communism which once led us to embrace any dictator who joined us in that fear."

Indicative of the new approach was the revelation of a top-secret strategic study (called PRM-10) in which the President's key advisers, including Zbigniew Brzezinski, suggested conceding one third of Germany if the Soviets attacked Western Europe, advised against stepped-up defense spending and urged a program of economic assistance to the Soviets as a method of averting the risks of war.

Also suggestive is the war against our intelligence and internal security agencies, including crippling restrictions on the CIA and abolition of the President's Foreign Intelligence Advisory Board. As noted by Leo Cherne, former chairman of the FIAB, the constraints and guidelines currently imposed on our intelligence services make it difficult if not impossible to head off terrorism or counter the far-flung activities of the Soviet KGB—which routinely infringes the privacy of U.S. citizens, and threatens their security, without a peep from the usual protectors of our "civil liberties" in Washington.

Most indicative of all is the stance adopted by Carter himself in the realm of arms control. As Thomas W. Wolfe of the Rand Corporation put it: "With regard to strategic weapons, it appeared that the favored line was one of constraints upon the pace, and in some cases the existence, of programs inherited from the previous administrations." In rapid order, Carter deferred development of the MX missile (subsequently revived to help promote adoption of SALT II), cancelled the B-1 bomber, renounced the so-called "neutron bomb," slowed development of the Trident submarine, and shut down production of the Minuteman missile.

As pointed out by the Administration's top arms control consultant, the object of the Carter policy was to make sure we did *not* possess a strategic advantage over Moscow. "Even if the U.S. could obtain strategic superiority," said Brzezinski SALT consultant Victor Utgoff, "it would not be desirable because I suspect we would throw our weight around in some very risky ways. . . . *It is in the U.S. interest to allow the few remaining areas of our strategic advantage to slip away."* (Italics added.)

This view of the global situation was enshrined by Carter in the SALT II treaty, which would lock the United States into a situation of permanent inferiority in many weapons categories (for instance, it permits the Soviets to have 308 so-called "heavy" missiles while we have none).

SALT II represents the triumph of a tiny coterie of academic theoreticians who have been working since the early 1960s to promote the view that there should be a "balance of terror" between the United States and U.S.S.R. In this view, nuclear war can best be avoided if each side is *exposed* to nuclear obliteration—which means there should be no defense of civilian populations from nuclear attack. This theory is called "mutual assured destruction," or MAD.

It is in obedience to MAD that, over the years, we have abandoned our anti-missile defenses and air interceptors, refused to pursue a program of civil defense and introduced deliberate inaccuracies into our offensive weapons so that they can't knock out the Soviets' missiles—all to reassure the Kremlin through our complete defenselessness. Unfortunately, there is no evidence that Moscow has accepted our invitation to compete in terms of self-inflicted weakness. (In belated recognition of this fact, there has been a reported move in recent months to abandon MAD as the basis of U.S. missile targeting.)

In keeping with PRM-10, the Carter regime has funneled vast amounts of U.S. technology to the Kremlin, including energy-producing equipment, computers needed for management of missiles and other modern military forces, ball-bearing machinery required for the guidance of MIRVs and a vast amount of industrial equipment needed to gear up a modern military machine. Symbolic of this process is the gigantic Kama River truck plant—built for Moscow with hundreds of millions of dollars' worth of our technology—whose products rolled into Afghanistan with Soviet combat troops on board.

While these strategic moves have been occurring, we have simultaneously been following the IPS scenario by stiff-arming former allies and putting out the welcoming mat for Marxist revolutionaries. We have focused our "human rights" agitation on such IPS targets as South Korea and Chile (ignoring North Korea and Cuba), given the back of our hand to anti-communist Taiwan, helped topple a pro-Western black majority government in Zimbabwe-Rhodesia and the Somoza regime in Nicaragua—and then rushed to lavish aid on Marxist successor governments in both these nations.

Put it all together and it is apparent that the Carter Administration has been pursuing the IPS–"new establishment" scenario with a vengeance in virtually every category of defense and foreign policy. Again, the leverage of a small band of ideologues on the public policy process of an otherwise rudderless federal government is impressive. As with our domestic affairs, these ideologues have moved into a policy vacuum created by an atmosphere of politics-as-usual and public ignorance of what the government is doing.

Our foreign default is linked to our domestic troubles as well by the insatiable desire of our politicians to play the game of domestic handouts—which have been substantially financed by siphoning money from defense. In the aftermath of Vietnam, the national mood of retreat from global leadership was made to order for those who wanted to cut back on defense outlays and jack up spending on "human needs," according to the program laid out by IPS.

In 1968, at the height of the Vietnam conflict, the defense outlay of the United States amounted to 45 percent of the federal budget and 9.7 percent of the Gross National Product. A decade later, in 1979, defense was down to 23 percent of the budget and 5.1 percent of GNP. In terms of constant dollars, the defense budget was $30 billion *smaller* in 1979 than it had been in 1968. In the meantime, federal spending generally, and welfare spending in particular, was skyrocketing—which means that we have been financing a domestic orgy of bread and circuses at the expense of our national security requirements.

The point of all this, allegedly, has been to reassure the communists of our good intentions and to induce them to follow us in conciliatory behavior. As recent history and the grimly changing map of the world all too clearly indicate, it hasn't worked. Instead, as noted by Carter's own chairman of the Joint Chiefs of Staff, General David Jones, the Soviet arms buildup has accelerated precisely during the period of our restraint as part of the "SALT process."

By the same token, Moscow's invasion of Afghanistan, the Soviet-Cuban advance through Africa and communist triumphs in Latin America have all occurred while the "new establishment" and the Carter Administration have been trying out their theories of peace-through-weakness. There has never been an iota of evidence that the communists can be bought off in this fashion, and there is no evidence of it today.

From time to time in the Cold War, when confronted by strength or a tactical advantage to be gained through peaceful rhetoric, the Soviets have beat a temporary retreat—only to come surging back when they felt the time was ripe for new aggression. Their basic rule was well expressed by Lenin: Probe with the bayonet until you meet steel, then withdraw. In their continued probing of American resolve under Jimmy Carter and the "new establishment," the Soviets have met only flab—and a blind unwillingness to face the global facts of life.

It is doubtful that, within our lifetimes, the United States has ever faced a peril as great as it faces today. Confronted by an implacable enemy which has never relented in its determination to bury us and is moving swiftly to encompass our defeat, we find our national policies being set by a coterie of defeatists and dream-world theoreticians who tell us the dangers that beset us are the fault of America and its allies and their "inordinate fear of communism." Our dwindling defenses and continuing capitulations around the globe are the inevitable consequences of this sophisticated folly.

Abroad even more than on the home front, the survival of our nation is in jeopardy. It cannot be assured unless we break the death grip of the "new establishment" on our defense and foreign policies and reassert the authority of the American people over the course of national conduct in the world arena.

X

An Agenda for Action

We are not weak if we make proper use of the means which the God of Nature has placed in our power.

—PATRICK HENRY

On first appraisal, much of this book involves the topics of economics and finance. But the basic problem confronting us is actually political—more precisely, the impact of politics on our economic system, our lives, our families, our freedoms. Unless we come to terms with the political problem, and free our nation from the yoke of political interference, the so-called economic questions can never be resolved.

Inflation, for example, is not an "economic issue"—it is a moral, intellectual and political issue that has devastating economic and social consequences. We must deal with it, as with our other difficulties, at the moral-political level first. We must confront the long-range implications of what we are doing to ourselves and realize that, unless we control inflation now, we face the prospect of rampaging hyper-inflation, with all the evils that entails, and a disastrous depression.

We need to study the example of that courageous leader, Margaret Thatcher. She has understood the crucial importance of controlling inflation, slowing the rapid growth of government and freeing the British economy from stifling controls. She has also understood that such a course is not an easy one, that it involves painful choices and hard decisions in this era of something-for-nothing expectations. And she has stuck to her guns despite predictable outcries and political pressures. As she put it in a recent address: "We don't shrink from any tasks. We shall not stop, however hard the road."

That is the spirit we need in America today. It has frequently been said that, in the growth of government power and the resulting weakness of national performance, we suffer from "the British disease"—since Britain went through this series of afflictions first. Now, perhaps, we can benefit from "the British cure" prescribed by Mrs. Thatcher—if we have the courage to adopt it.

If anything is plain from recent history, it is that the evils which beset us are not inevitable, fated in the nature of things or imposed upon us by events. On the contrary, our economic collapse at home and woeful default in foreign dealings have been the result of human error and indecision, stemming from mistaken philosophies, political trimming and tunnel vision on the part of our alleged leaders.

Most of all, our gravest problems at this hour result from the power exerted over public policy by a handful of exotic theoreticians who have lost all faith in America, its traditional ideals and its future as a free

society. Driven by ideological passions, these defeatists have imposed a "no-growth" posture on the
United States economy and mapped out a strategy of
impotence and abdication for us in our foreign dealings.

It goes without saying that any true reform of
American government aiming at the revival of our
national spirit must begin by cleaning these people
out of policy-making roles in government and by restoring political authority to its rightful lodgement
with the people. If the no-growth counterculture and
new establishment continue to work their will in
Washington, America as a free society is doomed.

Ridding our government of these defeatists, however, would be only the bare beginnings of an answer
to our problems. These ideologues have been able to
impose their influence on the nation because there has
been a total vacuum of leadership in Washington—
an aimless drift of politics-as-usual, devoid of principle or long-range purpose. As long as that vacuum
exists, the best America can possibly hope for is to
tumble toward oblivion at a slightly slower rate of
speed.

What is urgently needed is an agenda for reform:
a clear-cut set of policy objectives for the restoration
of American greatness at home and abroad and a series
of policy steps that will move us consistently toward
their fulfillment. Simply denouncing the evils of the
time and demanding that pernicious influences on our
government desist may be emotionally satisfying but
offers little by way of concrete remedy for our ills.
We need measures that will right the situation and
prevent recurrence of our crippling ailments in the
future.

Such reform, admittedly, is not an easy task. In

fact, I sometimes wonder if the deterioration in our society has gone so far that reversal is impossible—not so much in terms of practical steps that might be taken but in public willingness and patience to accept them. History tells us that when social and intellectual dissolution has reached a certain stage, it becomes difficult if not impossible to reverse. In my more pessimistic moments, I fear that this may be the case with the United States.

On the other hand, our most deeply cherished values and the lessons of our heritage tell us that such historical defeatism is mistaken. It is our moral determination and our vision that define the scope of what we can accomplish; we are not determinists whose course of action is dictated by some unalterable force or by the implacable pressure of events. We are a free people, with the power to decide our destiny. We *can* correct the evils that afflict us if we have the intelligence to see what must be done and the courage to take the necessary action.

Among the most difficult changes we will have to make are those that are needed on the home front. We must restore the vitality of our economy, retool our industrial machinery, regain control of our energy destiny, lift stifling regulation, bring government spending and taxing under control and end the nightmare of runaway inflation—create in the American people a New Spirit of Enterprise. In any country that has gone this far down the road to the welfare state, a reversal of the policies that have produced such evils is difficult to accomplish. But unless we do reverse them, we face the prospect of financial collapse and economic ruin. I propose a half dozen urgently needed reforms:

1. We must bring the federal budget into balance.

The chronic something-for-nothing deficits of the past 20 years, creating massive pressures toward inflation, must be brought to a halt. The federal government must start living within its means. Allowance can be made for emergencies and for temporary deficits at times of recession, but over the course of the business cycle the budget must be balanced. I would favor a constitutional amendment to this effect, since legislative efforts to achieve a balance have proved so totally ineffective in the past.

2. While helping to stem the tide of inflation, a balanced budget is not a be-all and end-all in itself. It is theoretically possible to balance the budget at 50 or 60 percent of GNP by raising taxes, which would defeat the goal of freeing our economy from the downward drag of massive government spending. It is the total burden of government that is the ultimate evil, not simply the method by which it is financed. I therefore favor a constitutional amendment to limit federal spending, placing a ceiling on total federal outlays however funded (including off-budget items, federal credits and federal loan guarantees) as a percent of GNP.

3. By the same token, I would urge a series of actions to reduce tax rates on personal, business and investment income. The American people must have relief from the present crushing burden of taxation. This is important not only as part of a strategy to reduce the aggregate weight of government on the economy but to restore incentives to work, invest and produce—incentives now negated by high marginal tax rates. Such reductions will go a long way toward restoring our vanished productivity. They should be phased in, however, to coincide with projected reductions in the rate of spending growth to help ensure

the balancing of our national accounts.

4. In keeping with a new policy of fiscal restraint, we must establish firm guidelines for the conduct of monetary policy—which has been the principal source of our runaway inflation. In an era of double-digit price hikes, we can no longer tolerate a situation in which the supply of money grows at double the rate of GNP, sending more and more dollars in pursuit of the existing volume of goods and services. I would suggest a growth rate of two to four percent annually for the monetary base, in keeping with the long-term trend in productivity and real output.

5. The rogue elephant of bureaucracy must be brought under control. The power of bureaucratic agencies to serve arbitrarily and simultaneously as prosecutor, judge and executioner must be ended. And the do-it-now-and-damn-the-consequences attitude embedded in current regulatory law and the mind-set of too many regulators must be curtailed. A practical rule for doing this would be obligatory "economic impact" or cost-benefit findings before a regulation goes into effect—and only if the benefits exceed the costs may the regulation be adopted.

6. Literally crucial is the subject of energy. We can no longer afford to live in an energy lotus land where government holds energy prices below their market levels, blocks construction of energy facilities and denies access to energy resources, yet somehow makes us "energy independent"! We need energy deregulation across the board—including oil and natural gas prices, reasonable rules for the mining and burning of coal, a go-ahead on nuclear power and an end to the lock-up of Alaskan and other Western lands, permitting reasonable prospecting with due regard for the environment.

Adoption of such policies* would go a long way toward restoring the productive power and vibrancy of our economy, resulting in more and better jobs for American citizens, higher real incomes and an end to the silent but ruinous incursions of inflation. By reestablishing our economic vitality and ensuring the soundness of our currency, these domestic reforms would also go far toward refurbishing our tarnished image in the world arena. Additional steps are obviously needed, however, to undo the deadly peril of our current global situation.

Oddly enough, the dangers which confront us in the realm of foreign policy are, in some respects, more easily handled than those which plague us on the home front. Not that the Soviet Union and the danger that it poses are going to fade away or that we are going to escape the rigors of the Cold War struggle at any time in the foreseeable future. For America and its allies, the world is going to be an extremely hazardous place for many years to come.

The steps that must be taken to shore up our ramparts against this danger, however, are relatively clear—and, given an informed public, should command a fair degree of popular support. They are clear because they are rooted in obvious common sense, outrageously flouted in the present conduct of our foreign policy. We simply need to restore a modicum

---

*Also, I would urge one underlying structural change which, in my opinion, would alter the constant vote-buying focus of too much policy-making in Washington: My experience in government and observation of every administration since World War II persuade me that our system would work much better, and officeholders would function more effectively in the public interest, if we amended the Constitution to limit Presidents to a single six-year term and members of Congress to no more than 12 consecutive years of service.

of sanity to our conduct overseas—to *stop* doing the criminally stupid things we have been doing to weaken our defenses, destroy our allies, and build up our enemies.

I will leave to those who are specialists in the strategic and technical subtleties of defense the fine points of what should be done to upgrade our military hardware. On a common sense reading of what is happening in the world, however, and on the obvious imperatives of survival, I offer the following six-point program for the protection of our national interests and the restoration of our global leadership:

1. We must renounce the delusion that the Soviets are "mellowing," don't really mean it when they say they will "bury" us, or somehow commit their aggressions and atrocities because we make them nervous. Communist doctrine and the unbroken record of more than half a century indicate that the U.S.S.R. is committed to a program of conquest and subversion, with America as its ultimate target, and we would be well advised to proceed on that assumption until we have some evidence to the contrary.

2. We must pull our heads out of the sand of neo-isolationism and reassert our role as leaders of the free world and be prepared to make the tough decisions required of leaders. The grim truth is that unless America takes the lead against the Soviets, the job will not get done. There is no one else to do it. If we renounce our responsibility for this task with all that it implies in terms of human freedom, global peace and national honor, we will deserve the contempt of future generations for cowardice and moral failure.

3. We must move rapidly to repair the sagging state of our defenses—including better missiles, a new manned bomber and anti-missile defenses. The in-

credible folly of "MAD" must be rejected, as must the one-sided series of concessions that have been made to Moscow in the SALT II process. We can negotiate a SALT agreement, but the negotiations must be from strength, not weakness, and they must be conducted on terms that protect our national security and vital interests.

4. We must start supporting our friends and stop supporting our enemies. The lunacy of undercutting friendly governments on the hypocritical pretext of "human rights"—facilitating the triumph of those who would destroy *all* human rights—must end forthwith. The list of former allies who have been toppled in recent years with the assistance or acquiescence of our State Department is truly appalling.

5. We must stop building the Soviet war machine with critical infusions of our technology. Through the Orwellian illogic of the MAD theoreticians, we are in the lunatic posture of creating a balance of power *against ourselves*—weakening our own strategic arsenal while building the economic and military strength of our opponents. Much of the threat that Moscow poses to us could be reduced if this policy were ended—and if all commerce with the Eastern bloc were conducted on the basis of *quid pro quo* (such as halting the subjugation of Afghanistan). Also, we need much closer coordination with our allies to ensure that our trading policies are sensible and consistent in protecting free world interests.

6. We must take a series of steps to reassert concern for our security and national sovereignty. Our crippled intelligence and internal security agencies, which are a vital part of our defenses, must be restored to operation. And, I am now convinced, we must reinstitute the draft. I was one of those who favored

the experiment with the volunteer army, but I am sad to say the experiment hasn't worked. Both symbolically and substantively, the return of the draft would signal to the Russians the resolve of the American people to protect our nation's security and to bear the burden of global leadership.

Finally, a more general point concerning America's posture in today's disorderly and dangerous world: We must rid ourselves of the crippling notion that our global mission is somehow to be *liked*—to "reassure" our adversaries in the Kremlin, to be guided by the latest enthusiasm of "world opinion" and other similar nonsense. This is the moral equivalent of conducting our domestic policies according to the latest poll results—only more so.

In dealing with our allies, our goal should not be popularity but respect, based on firm, dependable and honest conduct. In dealing with our adversaries, our goal should be not only respect but, in certain circumstances, fear—fear that, if aggression is committed, freedom threatened or American citizens manhandled, a swift and sure response will be forthcoming. Only such a posture, credibly backed by the strength to enforce it, can keep the peace against aggressors.

It is not the fate of great powers to be loved or liked, and if we behave as responsible leaders in the years to come, we probably won't be very popular with the despots in the Kremlin or the "third world" noisemakers at the United Nations. Too bad. By acting with the responsible firmness and determination that befit our station in the world, however, we will be respected.

In all our affairs, domestic as well as foreign, it is a time for action—a time for renewal of the American spirit. Enterprise, thrift and self-reliance can be reborn in the United States if we adopt a plan of action based on common sense, rather than on utopian theories or child-like evasion of our duties. The long run is here, and the bills are rapidly falling due. We must face the economic facts of life. We must make the hard decisions that they require of us. And, with God's help, we will be free.

Index

Mobil, 69
Monetary policy, 20
need for guidelines, 137
Money supply ("M1"), 35n
Moorhead, William, 29
Moose, Richard, 126
Morgenthau plan, 116–17
Morley, Christopher, 93
Mortgage rates, rise in, 4, 32
Moynihan, Daniel P., 55n
Mozambique, 9, 9n, 120, 122
Muhammad Reza Shah
Pahlevi, Shah of Iran,
121, 122

Nader, Ralph, 44, 89
Namibia, 121
National Association of Home
Builders, 87
National debt, 19, 20
ceiling, 32n
total, 5
National Highway Traffic
Safety Administration,
30
Natural gas
controls, 113, 137
reserves, 4, 111
NBC, 62
Netherlands, The, 7
Nevada, 113
Newsweek, 59
New York Times, 63, 66n,
69, 78n, 125n
Nicaragua, 8, 9, 9n, 71–72,
121, 122, 123, 129
Nixon, Richard M., 39–40,
100, 110
No-growth counterculture
crusaders, 45–49,
52–56, 63, 64, 73, 87,

93, 109, 112, 115
and courts, 55
and legislation, 55
North Korea, 121
Nuclear power, 4, 86, 111,
137
media coverage of, 64–66
opponents, 44, 45
Nuclear weapons,
maintenance of, 8

Occupational Safety and
Health Administration
(OSHA), 52, 89, 90
"Off-budget" spending, 26,
31–32
Office of Minority Enterprise,
30
Oil
import fee, 34
price controls, 33, 68,
110, 137
prices, and inflation, 34n
production controls,
111–13
reserves, 4, 109–11
Oil company profits, 66–69,
68n
"On Company Business"
(television series), 73
OPEC, 34, 114

Pakistan, 7, 123
Panama, 9
Panama Canal treaties, 8
media coverage of, 72–73
Passbook interest rate
regulation, 81, 81n,
104
Patriotism, 13